The

SCIATICA
HANDBOOK

A Practical Guide to Understanding, Treating and Preventing Sciatica and Back Problems

by
Bill Habets

Copyright © MMX The Windsor Group

Typeset by SJ Design and Publishing, Bromley, Kent.

Published MMX by The Windsor Group,
Hamilton House,
2 Station Road,
Epping CM164HA

ISBN 978-1-903-904-30-5

Table of Contents

4

Foreword

It is a great shame that literally millions of people have the quality of their lives impaired by different kinds of back pain, especially as these are problems which in many instances can quite easily be controlled or eased by some relatively simple remedies or treatments. As you'll discover later in this book, there are also numerous ways through which sufferers can help themselves, this self-help quite often being sufficient to bring about complete relief from the symptoms in many cases.

Of course, while there are many things you can do yourself to prevent, reduce and even perhaps totally eliminate back pain and sciatica, it must be stressed that you should *always seek your doctor's advice if your symptoms are either severe or frequent*. A book like this can never be – nor is it intended to be – in any way a substitute for professional advice. You are therefore strongly urged always to consult your own doctor before trying out any treatment other than that which has been prescribed for you. Please also note that the word 'treatment' in this instance is to be taken at its widest possible interpretation, including such things as making changes to your diet, trying out new exercises, in fact doing anything that could have a bearing on your health. Only your own doctor can help you decide what is the most appropriate treatment in the very specific circumstances of your personal situation.

I'd also like to make a point about style: in this book, you'll find many sentences in which the male pronoun 'he' is used even when, within the context, it's equally possible that the person referred to is a woman. Some writers get around this problem by using phrases like 'he/she' or 'he or she', or alternatively by using the plural pronoun 'they'. In my view, all of these solutions can be awkward and even possibly distracting to the reader. For these reasons, I've opted for simplicity and readability instead, asking you to mentally change the masculine pronoun to its female form whenever that should be necessary.

In closing, I'd like to say a sincere 'thank you' to all those experts and organisations who have given so generously of their time and experience during my research.

Bill Habets

NOTICE

This book and the views, opinions and advice expressed in it should not be used as a substitute or relied upon for medical diagnosis. You are advised always to consult your doctor or other qualified medical practitioner for specific information and advice upon health matters. Whilst every effort has been made to ensure accuracy, the publisher cannot accept responsibility or liability for the information set out in this book, nor for any of the opinions or advice expressed therein.

CHAPTER 1

What is sciatica?

An extremely common condition that's estimated to affect millions of people every day, sciatica can be broadly defined as a pain or other unpleasant or disturbing sensation that is generally felt in one or more of the following areas of the body: the lower back, the buttocks, the outer sides of the thigh and calf, the feet, and toes.

Two key points about sciatica:

1) The name 'sciatica' describes a symptom, not a specific disease nor even necessarily the *exact* underlying cause that leads to the pain; and

2) The areas where the pain is felt are not an indication of where the cause of it originates – sciatica almost invariably stems from trouble in the back, whether or not any pain is experienced there as well.

Sciatica, in fact, is just one of the many symptoms that can mark different kinds of back problems, or more specifically problems affecting the spine.

Although spinal problems and sciatica are directly linked as cause and effect, this relationship is often less than obvious when a sufferer first experiences sciatica, especially when the pain or discomfort is relatively mild and perhaps only present for a very short time. Identifying the cause of the pain is made even more confusing at times because:

- Sciatic pain – wherever it occurs and whatever form it takes – is not necessarily accompanied by back pain of any kind; and
- Back pain – even that resulting from the very kind of spinal problems that normally give rise to sciatica – is not necessarily accompanied by sciatica.

To add extra confusion, sciatic pain potentially manifests itself not only in many different places but also in a wide variety of ways and degrees of intensity. At one extreme, sciatica may be no more than an occasional light tingle that's sensed rather than felt in some part of the buttocks, legs, or feet; at the other extreme, it is a searing, wrenching, agonising pain that affects most of the leg and can become truly disabling. It is in the nature of sciatica that it frequently comes and goes for no obviously discernible reason, at times disappearing of its own accord for days, weeks or even months, then to perhaps eventually return with a vengeance.

While the relationship between some kinds of sciatic pain and spinal problems is often less than obvious at first, equally obscure can be the reason why sciatica may be experienced by a sufferer at certain times but not at others. However, apart from any underlying spinal condition that may be responsible for bringing on sciatica, there are many additional causes that could be described as 'secondary' in that they have been identified as likely to trigger sciatica, no matter how good your spine may have been in the first place. Common examples of these contributing factors include:

- Poor posture – how you stand and sit affects how well your spine, no matter its condition, will be able to cope with the demands you place upon it.
- An incident that suddenly, perhaps only very briefly, placed a much greater than usual strain upon the spine – this could be because of being involved in an accident, falling down or slipping, or just merely lifting something heavy or bending down awkwardly.
- The cumulative effect of strain upon the spine – such as resulting from frequently driving long distances or spending hours hunched over a desk. Cumulative strain can contribute to sciatica in two separate but connected ways: first, it can cause one of the specific spinal conditions whose symptoms include sciatica; secondly, once such a condition exists, it can make it worse, so that sciatica if not present previously, now manifests itself.

- Whether you're overweight – it's obvious that the heavier you are, the more weight your spine has to support. It also follows that the poorer the condition of your spine, the greater is likely to be any harmful effect that being overweight will impose upon it.

THE PHENOMENON OF REFERRED PAIN

Just how difficulties in the back cause sciatic pain – this being a typical example of what is called 'referred pain' (medical name: *synalgia*), that is a pain that occurs in a part of the body other than where it might have been expected – will be explained in full in the next chapter. In the meantime, let us briefly note that referred pain is quite a common phenomenon: for example, we all know that some heart disorders can cause pain in the left arm and fingers. Equally, an abscess below the diaphragm may lead to referred pain in the shoulders. The confusion created by referred pain stems from the fact that the sensory nerves from different parts of the body share common pathways when they reach the spinal cord. To treat any referred pain successfully, its origin must be located first, because that's where the treatment will have to be effective to bring about permanent relief.

It follows from this that the treatment of sciatica must ultimately be addressed to its source, and this is invariably in the spine, and not where the pain may manifest itself. Having said that, some local treatments applied to the site of the pain – such as heat or gentle massage – can be extremely useful in reducing its severity, but these approaches will only reduce the pain temporarily, not cure it or improve its root cause. Nevertheless, *palliatives* – the name given to treatments that relieve or soothe the symptoms of a disease or disorder without effecting a cure – can be of great help. Pain-killing medicines, such as aspirin or paracetamol, are essentially palliatives, their effect limited either to making the pain disappear or at least lessening it, so that it becomes more bearable. Such simple remedies can, however, have an extremely important role to play in the management of sciatica, especially when the symptoms are fairly mild and/or occur but rarely and the main purpose of treatment is to stop them from interfering with the tasks of daily life.

WHY IT'S CALLED SCIATICA

The word 'sciatica' derives from the term *sciatic nerve*. Sciatic pain is a very specific kind of referred pain, one that is experienced at one or more places along the course of the sciatic nerve, which is the major nerve of the leg (and, incidentally, the nerve with the largest diameter in the human body). The sciatic nerve – one for each leg, of course – starts at the lower end of the spine and continues down behind the thigh. Directly above the knee joint, the sciatic nerve divides into two main branches – the *tibial* and *common peroneal* nerves – one branch travelling down the shin to the big toe, and the other running down the back of the calf to the heel before it winds around to the front of the foot and then extends into the toes.

The above is, of course, but a simplified description of the sciatic nerves; if you were to look in *Gray's Anatomy*, the classic volume that still remains a standard medical reference nearly 150 years after it was first published, you'd find that more than four pages of small type are devoted to listing all the intricate sub-divisions of these nerves. While little purpose would be served by going into all this detail, it is important to note that almost any part of the leg can be affected by sciatic pain.

TYPICAL FORMS OF SCIATIC PAIN

As already noted briefly, sciatica can be experienced in a number of ways. Most typically it manifests itself as one or more of the following sensations, with some sufferers having more than one kind of sciatic pain or discomfort:

- A pain that sufferers describe as 'aching', 'stinging', or even 'burning', this either following a specific course, such as along the back of the leg, or restricted to one specific area, such as the upper part of the thigh.

- A cramping pain, as though the muscles in the affected leg are contracting involuntarily. 'Cramping' sciatica is also often marked by spasms.

- Less specific – and also usually less severe – pains, including feelings of numbness, or experiencing 'pins and needles', these once again being experienced either over a fairly large area or concentrated within a much smaller one.

Because it's only too easy to mistake some of the pains or feelings of discomfort that arise from 'mild' sciatica for something else – for example, pins and needles or cramp may happen because you've been sitting too long in the same position, especially if your legs were crossed – it often takes some time before a sufferer comes to the conclusion that his symptoms are due to something specific and are more than merely the kind of odd sensations most of us experience now and then, dismissing them from our mind once they disappear seemingly of their own accord.

For many, however, the onset of sciatica is only too obvious as its pain is so intense that it is virtually crippling during its worst moments. A bad attack of sciatica can be so disabling that even the smallest movement, such as getting in or out of a chair, or even sneezing or coughing, brings on agonising distress. Acute sciatica can usually, but not always, be linked to some recent incident or event that provoked it.

The specific underlying causes of sciatica are examined in the next chapter in which we also look at the 'greater picture' of back pain in general.

CHAPTER 2

The spine and sciatica

As explained in the previous chapter, sciatica is a referred pain, one whose cause lies elsewhere than where it is felt, the source in this case invariably being in the back. As the only permanent way to deal with any symptom is to treat its cause, let us look more closely at the back and find out what can go wrong there to set off pain elsewhere in the body.

THE SPINE AND ITS VERTEBRAE

The human spine – also at times called the spinal column, vertebral column, or just the backbone – is a flexible bony column that extends from the base of the skull to the small of the back. It serves two main purposes:

- Working together with various muscles and 'girdles' – the latter being encircling or arching arrangements of bones, such as the pelvic and shoulder girdles – the spine provides the support that enables us to stand upright.
- It also encloses – and so protects to a large extent – the spinal cord, that portion of the central nervous system whose nerve cells and bundles connect all parts of the body with the brain.

Structurally, the spine consists of a number of vertebrae (or individual bones) that are stacked on top of each other and separated as well as connected by discs of fibrocartilage (the intervertebral discs, which are discussed later in this chapter).

Although adults have 26 vertebrae, new-born babies have 33, nine of those extra ones becoming eventually fused into two separate single bones. An adult spine has five regions, consisting of the following, and starting from the bottom up:

- Four fused coccygeal – or tail – vertebrae, which together make up the coccyx.
- Five fused sacral vertebrae, which form the sacrum.
- Five lumbar – or lower back – vertebrae.
- Twelve thoracic (also at times called *thoriac*) – or chest – vertebrae.
- Seven cervical – or neck – vertebrae.

GREAT ENGINEERING BUT POOR DESIGN

That the human spine can cope so well most of the time with all the demands that are placed upon it is truly a marvel, especially when you consider that its basic design leaves much to be desired. Reduced to its essentials, the spinal column consists of a bunch of building-blocks placed on top of each other and held together by various ligaments and muscles that collectively act somewhat like the guy-ropes that keep a tent up. To make matters worse, not only are the building-blocks not piled neatly and directly one upon the other, they in fact are arranged in curves and bulges, making the whole structure all that more unstable. Additionally, of course, the whole thing has to be able to perform and withstand a whole range of bending, twisting and stretching movements, the muscular guy-ropes keeping it all working smoothly through exerting various carefully balanced forces. As anatomists are wont to remark in appreciation, the spine is, "Truly great engineering . . ."

Great engineering it may be, but the spine is also poorly designed in that it really is a makeshift arrangement that originally wasn't meant to do the job it has to do in humans. While the theory of evolution is still hotly debated by some, it is nowadays generally accepted that man's earliest predecessors walked on four legs instead of two. When a two-legged stance evolved gradually, this was accompanied by major changes in the spine. While these alterations were good enough to enable us to stand and walk in an upright position, the spine's essential design remained much the same with the net result that it has a number of built-in potential flaws, many of which are responsible for the prevalence of back problems.

While the overall good health of the spine is vital to anyone, the part of it of particular concern for people suffering from sciatica is the lower back, the reason for this being that this is where the lumbar spinal nerves join with the sacral nerves from the spinal cord to form the sciatic nerves.

THE INTERVERTEBRAL DISCS

These are flexible plates of fibrocartilage that connect any two adjacent vertebrae in the spine, between them accounting for a fifth to a quarter of the length of the spinal column. Each disc has two main parts:

- In the centre of the disk is the *nucleus pulposus*, a gelatinous substance; and
- Surrounding the centre is a ring of very strong fibrocartilage – the *annulus fibrosus* – whose outer edges are made of collagen, making it much stronger than most other ligaments in the body.

Apart from connecting the vertebrae in a flexible manner, the discs also serve as a series of shock absorbers that help protect the spinal cord and the brain from the effects of impact resulting from the body's movements. For example, were it not for the discs, the impact produced just by walking would send shock waves directly through a more or less rigid spine directly to the brain where damage would eventually result.

Two key points to note about intervertebral discs:

- The younger you are, the more effective they are as shock absorbers. At birth, the nucleus pulposus is extremely elastic, but as you grow older, this jelly-like centre becomes harder, some of its gelatinous substance having been replaced by cartilage.
- Apart from any natural deterioration that accompanies ageing,

the discs can also become damaged by accident or disease. One all too common occurrence is a prolapsed intervertebral disc (often simply referred to as PID, or a 'slipped disc'), a condition in which the pulpy inner material of a disc protrudes through the fibrous outer ring. When this happens the protruding material can exert pressure on adjoining nerve roots and ligaments, and should this pressure affect the roots of the sciatic nerves, then one or more of the typical sciatic pains may follow.

As far as what causes a disc to *prolapse* – incidentally, this word simply means the falling down or slipping out of place of an organ or a part of the body – this is usually the result of one of two scenarios:

- As part of the natural wear and tear that marks ageing, the outer ring of a disc will gradually have become weaker and weaker until one day it is so weak that the smallest amount of extra pressure upon it allows part of the gelatinous centre to pass through it. The final precipitating incident that causes a disc's prolapse may be quite minor – such as an awkward bending or twisting movement, or even a sneeze or a cough – and would not have had any repercussions were the disc's outer ring not already very weak. In many ways, this can be described as an accident waiting to happen. If a disc is so weak that it prolapses because of a sneeze, then it would have done so sooner or later.

- Alternatively, a disc may prolapse because it has been subjected to an unusually great amount of stress, such as can happen during a fall or a road accident. Naturally, the condition of the disc will to some extent dictate whether it prolapses or not in given circumstances, but any disc, no matter how healthy and resilient, can fail when subjected to enough force.

While a prolapsed disc is one of the major causes of sciatica, there are also several others, including:

- **A disc that's become distorted or bulges**. Without actually prolapsing, an intervertebral disc may just change shape sufficiently, usually because it's affected by nearby muscles in spasm,

15

so that it's flattened, part of its squeezed out section creating pressure on the nerves.

- Various **rheumatic diseases** can attack the spinal joints, causing them to swell, so putting pressure on the nerves.
- **Osteoporosis** – a disorder that causes the loss of bony tissue, resulting in bones that are brittle and liable to fracture – can damage the vertebrae, one possible consequence of this damage being pressure upon the nerves.
- **Ankylosing spondylitis** – the first word describes a process of fusion of the bones across a joint space and the second means 'stiffening' – is a disorder in which the joints of the spine become inflamed. As the initial inflammation diminishes and healing takes place, extra bone may grow out from the sides of the vertebrae and can fuse these together, leading to a spine that's stiffened. Sciatica is a common symptom of the early stages of ankylosing spondylitis.
- **Spinal stenosis**. This is a condition in which the spinal canal has become narrowed.

As you can see from the above, the possible root-causes of sciatica are many and varied. While the symptomatic pain is usually due to a fairly straightforward problem that can generally be resolved through some simple remedies and precautions, there is always a possibility that a more serious disorder is responsible. For that reason, it is essential that sciatic pain that persists and fails to respond rapidly to rest and ordinary analgesics be investigated promptly and its cause fully established. Naturally, the way to find out what is causing *your* sciatica is to consult your doctor, something we'll look at in the next chapter.

CHAPTER 3

How your doctor can help you

As explained in the previous chapter, sciatica – whether or not it is also marked at times by pain or aches in the lower back – can stem from a wide variety of underlying problems, some of them potentially serious, others less so. However, no matter what your health problem may be, the first step towards a cure is, of course, to have it properly diagnosed.

Although you can probably judge fairly accurately whether sciatica is causing your symptoms, the only way to be sure that this is what is troubling you is to consult your doctor. Indeed, you should always seek medical advice if you're troubled by any kind of health difficulties that are either severe or occur frequently. Although almost everyone would agree with the preceding recommendation, it's nevertheless a fact that many people do have a great reluctance to seek help from the one quarter most qualified to provide it, their doctor, and will keep on finding reason after reason to postpone making an appointment.

Research into why so many people troubled by chronic symptoms fail to seek the help that's available found that this reluctance usually derived from one or more of the following reasons:

- Many patients postponed or altogether avoided consulting their doctor because they feared the diagnosis would bring bad news.
- Many others said they avoided seeking medical help because this would be to acknowledge that their problems were of more than just a temporary nature and unlikely to go away of their own accord.
- Sufferers were also put off because they had heard stories of how

people with similar-sounding symptoms eventually had to undergo complicated operations.

Should you, too, be someone who is hesitant about seeking medical help, let us look at the objections raised above one by one:

- *Postponing seeing your doctor because you fear that the news will be bad.*

Although a perfectly understandable reaction, this doesn't, however, serve your own interests best. First of all, the chances are that your doctor will find that your symptoms are evidence of a comparatively minor problem, one that can be cured or treated quite easily. Secondly, in the event that an operation is indicated, then it's usually best to have this done as soon as possible before your condition deteriorates further.

- *An unwillingness to acknowledge that your symptoms are going to remain with you unless they are treated.*

While most of us, when afflicted by symptoms that although troublesome are not that severe, may play a waiting game in the hope that the problem will go away of its own accord, you mustn't overdo this. If your symptoms are persistent or recurrent or are severe enough to cause you to be concerned about them, then you owe it to yourself to seek help, even if just for the sake of your own peace of mind.

- *You're put off from seeing your doctor because of what you've heard from other people with similar problems.*

Two thoughts to keep in mind: first, it's probable that the stories you heard were embellished in the telling; secondly, though the symptoms *sounded* similar, that doesn't mean that they were. Many different diseases can present themselves with remarkably similar symptoms, but the underlying causes – and therefore the treatments available and their rates of success – will vary tremendously.

As you can see from the above, there really are no good or logical reasons to keep on postponing consulting your doctor – and lots of good ones why you should do so just as soon as reasonably convenient! Remember that the sooner you get medical advice the

18

sooner you will learn what exactly is the matter with you, and the sooner you will be getting treatment which will make you feel better.

QUESTIONS YOUR DOCTOR MAY ASK

Once you've made an appointment to see your doctor, it's a good idea to spend a few minutes beforehand jotting some down quick notes about how your symptoms developed, so as to have the answer to any questions you may asked readily at hand. For example, try to recall when you first noticed any symptoms. Was the onset sudden or gradual? Did the pain go after a while, then keep coming back? Can you remember any particular incident that may have triggered its start? Are there some activities that you know will bring on the pain? What about things that make it worse or better? Also try to be clear in your mind about the exact site or sites of the pain, the path it may follow, and whether what you experience is best described as an aching, burning, searing, or tingling sensation. Naturally, if you also have back pain of any kind, then make similar notes about that as well.

During your consultation, your doctor – after having heard your account of your symptoms – will examine you. Just how thorough that first examination will be depends greatly upon whether the diagnosis in your case is a fairly obvious one. In most instances of simple sciatica, the doctor will quickly form a pretty accurate impression of what the cause of the trouble is, and, unless the symptoms are very severe, probably recommend that the first approach to be tried is a few days of rest, together with analgesics to control the pain. It is a standard principle of medicine that when several different treatments are possible, the first thing to try is the least invasive one. There are several good reasons for this:

- If the simple approach does the trick, all's well and good, and the patient will have been spared the risk of possible side-effects that more energetic approaches frequently entail; and

- As explained in greater detail further below, many instances of sciatica and back pain are essentially self-limiting; and
- Even tests and investigations can carry their own risks of side-effects.

A FEW NOTES ABOUT THE 'RESTING CURE'

Bed rest, although perhaps not seen as a treatment by some, still remains one of the best ways to deal with the symptoms of many kinds of back problems as this gives the body the opportunity to relax and bring its own recuperative abilities into play.

There has been a major change in professional opinion about how long someone with back pain should rest. It used to be that experts thought that a lengthy rest, one of perhaps several weeks, was essential to bring about recovery; nowadays, the general view is that a much shorter resting period – one to three days – is enough to allow the back to recuperate enough in most cases so that the patient should thereafter slowly become more active, although, of course, avoiding those activities known to worsen or trigger off back pain. Other points to note about the 'resting cure':

- Unless your doctor tells you so specifically (and you should ask if you have any doubt), do not interpret the word 'rest' as meaning 'bed rest'. Spending several days immobile in bed can at times be the very worst thing for some back sufferers. Rest means taking it easy and avoiding those tasks that involve a great deal of back movement. However, bed rest is more likely to be beneficial for sciatica sufferers than for those who have 'simple' back-ache, and it may be needed for longer, perhaps for a week or two.
- Resort to bed rest only if told to do so by your doctor.
- While 'resting' do some gentle – very, very gentle – exercises to keep your back moving, stopping these immediately if there's the slightest indication that they may be making things worse. Check carefully with your doctor what exercises will be safe and beneficial for you.
- As your symptoms begin to improve, graduate to somewhat more

20

energetic exercising, but still avoid any that place strain upon the back or involve a great deal of bending, lifting, stretching or twisting of the back. Walking at a moderate pace is an excellent form of exercising, as is swimming.

■ Take any prescribed medication – or use across-the-counter analgesics to keep the pain under control during the first few days. Paracetamol, aspirin and anti-inflammatory drugs, such as ibuprofen, may help.

■ Naturally, throughout your recovery period avoid all those activities that are likely to have brought on your problem in the first place – see *Chapter 7 – Tips to prevent back pain and sciatica* for useful recommendations and guidelines.

Many ordinary cases of sciatica and lower back pain will respond quite speedily to this regime, the symptoms usually beginning to reduce within a few days and thereafter perhaps taking up to six weeks or so to disappear completely. It's a fact that there is an incredibly high rate of 'spontaneous recovery' with many forms of back troubles, especially when the body is given a fair chance to bring its own self-healing powers into play.

Even sciatica that's due to a prolapsed disc often has a self-limiting course because that part of the disc's centre that protrudes from the outer ring eventually becomes deprived of nourishment and there-fore wastes away, so removing the pressure it had been creating on the nerve roots. How long the protruding material takes to wither away – and whether it leaves any residue – will affect how well the nerves recover eventually.

Naturally, should you be in that minority of sciatica and back pain sufferers whose symptoms do not respond sufficiently well to simple remedies, then you should return to see your doctor. At that time, he may suggest that you persevere a little longer with the current treatment, or if the symptoms remain reasonably severe and there is no improvement to speak of, he may well refer you to a specialist clinic at your local hospital for further diagnosis, as well as possible tests and investigations which are described in the next chapter.

CHAPTER 4

Investigations and surgical treatments

While the vast majority of instances of sciatica and lower back pain will respond to fairly simple treatment within a matter of weeks – or even much more quickly than that – there will always be some that will be more intractable, either not responding at all to just rest and analgesics or responding so little that it becomes evident that other treatments have to be considered. When that happens, a patient will usually be referred by his doctor to a specialist at the out-patient department of his local hospital.

Your initial consultation with a specialist will generally follow a similar pattern than when you first saw your own doctor: a history of the problem will be taken, additional questions will be asked, and there will be a further physical examination, this then probably followed by yet more questions.

At the end of your consultation, your specialist may well ask for various tests or other investigations to be done before making his diagnosis. Depending upon the circumstances, the purpose of these tests may be three-fold:

1) To specifically identify the cause of your troubles, if that's not already known; and
2) To eliminate other disorders which may be marked by similar symptoms; and
3) In those comparatively rare instances where an operation appears indicated, to help pinpoint exactly what approach is likely to work best.

Tests and investigations commonly used include:

- **X-rays.** While radiography is widely used in the diagnosis of many other disorders, its results are unfortunately often disappointing when back problems are being investigated, the difficulty being that many of the subtle changes in the spine that cause pain simply fail to show up clearly enough, especially during their early stages. Additionally, it takes a pretty large dose of radiation to X-ray the spine, and this is something that is best avoided unless truly indicated.

- **Computerised tomography (or CAT- or CT-scan).** Using much smaller doses of X-rays, this scanning method records the different thicknesses of tissues, translating these findings through the intermediary of a computer on to film that provides a cross-sectional image.

- **Magnetic resonance imaging (or MRI).** Producing images rather like those from a CAT-scan, this technique uses very powerful electromagnets instead of X-rays, so making it free of the risks that can accompany radiation.

- **Myelogram.** This is a specialised method of X-ray examination in which radio-opaque contrast medium is injected beforehand into the subarachnoid space in the spinal cord. Although this method is of particular value in recognising tumours of the spinal cord (as well as other conditions in which the cord or nerve roots are compressed), it needs to be accepted that this investigation represents a major intervention in itself and that therefore the patient should be made aware of the risks and side-effects that can be involved.

- **Blood tests.** These can provide information about a wide range of disorders, including many different types of rheumatic diseases.

While all these tests – and several others – are potentially available, it is highly unlikely that all will be requested or that even more than just one or two will be done.

WHAT NEXT?

Depending upon what the tests will have revealed, your consultant will probably suggest one of the following courses of action:

- To continue treating the problem conservatively for a while longer – that is with rest and analgesics – in the hope that this approach will still ultimately bring relief if only persevered with long enough.
- To use injections (see further below), either to possibly cure the underlying condition, or at least lessen the pain it produces.
- To refer you to a physiotherapist or other specialist so that mobilisation and manipulation techniques, coupled with a properly-devised exercise routine and pain management, will restore your back to health (see the next chapter for more information about the different kinds of treatments available).
- To refer you to another specialist, such as a rheumatologist (if your problems stem from a rheumatic disease), a neurologist (for problems involving the nervous system and the brain), or, should surgery be seen as a possibility, a neurosurgeon or orthopaedic surgeon.

WHETHER TO HAVE SURGERY OR NOT

Just because you're referred to a surgeon does not necessarily mean that an operation will be performed or even suggested. Surgeons will invariably make their own assessment of what they think is best. Although surgeons as a group do tend to have a bias towards their own speciality, they do also recognise that an operation is not always the best nor only answer. It is not rare for someone who was referred to a surgeon to then later on be referred to yet another specialist because the surgeon concluded that this was a case where less intrusive treatment might work just as well.

If surgery remains indicated, there are numerous possible procedures with an excellent track record. However, it also has to be pointed out that every form of surgery carries its own set of risks.

The decision to undergo an operation should therefore always be weighed up most carefully.

To help you make up your own mind about having an operation if one is offered, *The National Back Pain Association* suggests a number of questions you should ask your surgeon, these including:

- What is my exact diagnosis?
- Do I have signs of nerve root compression? And are the symptoms that I have directly related to nerve compression?
- What are my chances of good pain relief if I opt for a surgical intervention?
- Are there any alternatives to conventional surgery that I could try?
- How many of these procedures have you performed? What is your success rate for the surgery you have offered me?

What the NBPA is essentially saying through these suggestions is that any patient should make sure that the problem has been fully and accurately diagnosed, that an operation is likely to yield a good result, and that the surgeon is fully experienced in the intended procedure.

Additionally, the NBPA suggests that "the decision as to whether to have surgery and what type, is difficult, and needs very careful consideration. The only person who can really answer your questions about the effectiveness of surgery for your particular problem is your own surgeon. Ensure that you attend appointments well-prepared with your questions *written down* and, preferably, with someone else to listen to the response. *The Patient's Charter* states that *you have the right to any proposed treatment, including risks and alternatives, clearly explained before you decide whether or not to agree*".

A similar message comes from the Agency for Health Care Policy and Research, a part of the Department of Health and Human Services in the USA, which somewhat more bluntly states:

- Even having a lot of back pain does not by itself mean you need surgery.

25

- Surgery has been found to be helpful in only 1 in 100 cases of low back problems. In some people, surgery can even cause more problems. This is especially true if your only symptom is back pain.
- People with certain nerve problems or conditions such as fractures or dislocations have the best chance of being helped by surgery. In most cases, however, decisions about surgery do not have to be made right away.
- Most back surgery can wait for several weeks without making the condition worse.
- If surgery is recommended, be sure to ask about the reason for the surgery and about the risks and benefits you might expect.
- You may also want to get a second opinion.

SURGICAL PROCEDURES

The operation most commonly used in an effort to permanently cure back troubles caused by one or more discs is spinal fusion. Much more popular in the United States than in this country, this is an operation in which two or more vertebrae are essentially welded together and any troublesome discs between them removed. There are various ways of performing this procedure, but the one used most nowadays involves both anterior and posterior fusion of the vertebrae, the spine being approached from the front (via the abdomen) and then through the back. The damaged disc is then replaced by a bone graft.

Just how good the results of spinal fusion are is still a matter for debate by experts as the operation so far has not been the subject of a properly-controlled trial. Certainly, there are many patients who have benefited greatly from spinal fusion; in other instances, the results have been less favourable. More may be known in a year or two about the true benefits – and risks – of spinal fusion as a trial to compare its results with those achieved through non-surgical rehabilitation programmes is being set up.

Laser disc decompression is an alternative way of dealing with bulging discs that is currently being pioneered in America, but it also remains the subject of some controversy about just how effective and free from long-term side-effects it is.

This method has proven itself useful in dealing with a disc that bulges but where no part of the disc's soft centre is actually protruding from it, the pressure on the nerves resulting purely from the fact that the disc is larger than it would normally be.

Here's how this procedure is performed. A silicon optical fibre is temporarily inserted into the disc. Energy from a laser is transmitted into the disc via the fibre and this causes the loss of water and some of the substance that makes up the centre of the disc. As the pressure within the disc is decreased because of the loss of material, it shrinks and pulls the offending bulge off the nerve root, so decreasing or eliminating the pain.

The procedure takes about 15 to 30 minutes, followed by two to three hours in the recovery room. The advantages of this method is that operating time and hospitalisation is kept to a minimum, and that it can be suitable for patients who are surgical risks, for example, those with heart trouble or age-related problems. The proponents of this approach say that there have been no major complications to date and the degree of success is about 80 per cent so far.

OTHER PROCEDURES

Injections applied into the back can also help. Most of these injections contain two substances, an anaesthetic – to kill the pain – and steroids, to reduce inflammation. Some injections commonly used include:

- **Epidural injections.** These can bring almost instant relief as they numb the lining of the spinal cord, effectively stopping pain signals from getting through. While some patients find that a single injection cures the problem permanently, many others have to have them repeated frequently, perhaps as often as once a month. One possible good reason for having an epidural is that it can buy pain-free time during which the body's own natural healing process may rectify the underlying problem.

- **Nerve blocks.** These are applied directly into the root of the nerve that's causing the pain. Once again, response varies greatly: some patients only need one injection, others require frequent repeats.
- **Sclerosant injections.** The ligaments of the back are injected with a substance that irritates them, this irritation promoting the formation of new fibrous tissue. This therapy is mainly used in cases where vertebrae are damaged and grate against each other. Usually, it takes eight weeks or more before improvement is noticed as it takes time for the new tissue to form.

SUMMING IT UP

While an operation or other surgical procedure may be the only reasonable alternative eventually left open to some sufferers, it usually makes sense to first try other, less invasive avenues, leaving surgery as a last option.

Incidentally, should any of the above have made you apprehensive about your prospects, it's worth remembering in this context that:

- About half of the people suffering from nerve root pain recover within six weeks.
- Of those more stubborn cases that are referred by doctors to hospital out-patient departments, only one per cent of these will eventually require surgery.

CHAPTER 5

Other effective treatments for back pain and sciatica

While you should always first seek advice from your doctor if you're troubled by back symptoms, there are also many instances in which other therapies can be very helpful. In fact, your doctor may well refer you to a physiotherapist or, at times, suggest that you consult a practitioner of an alternative therapy as many of these have a proven track record in dealing very successfully with back problems.

The so-called 'other' treatments are normally divided into two main groups:

- The 'complementary' therapies that work alongside of and often as virtually part of conventional medicine; and
- The 'alternative' therapies which, as the label implies, offer an alternative to conventional medicine.

Although the distinction between the two types of therapies is usually quite clear, it can become somewhat blurred when looking solely at how effective some of these 'other' therapies can be in dealing with back problems. For example, the relatively little known Alexander Technique is usually considered to be an alternative therapy. However, because it concentrates upon posture, something that is so directly and obviously relevant to back troubles, this method is perhaps more 'complementary' than 'alternative' when it comes to difficulties involving the spine.

Rather than try to classify therapies as either complementary or alternative, it seemed more logical in this book to separate them into two groups depending upon how commonly they are employed in treating back problems. In this chapter you'll therefore find descriptions of the main 'other' therapies used to treat back problems while those that are still relevant but less so are listed separately in *Chapter 12 – More alternative treatments that can help.*

PHYSIOTHERAPY

If your doctor or hospital consultant refers you to a chartered physiotherapist – or you choose to see one independently – for back pain, the first step towards treatment will almost certainly be an in-depth assessment of your condition and what led to it. As well as an examination of your posture, this assessment will include a discussion that will cover your work and leisure activities, your history of back pain, the incident leading to the pain, and the nature and site of the pain.

Physiotherapy still remains largely a hands-on profession, and the most likely treatment for back pain will involve the physiotherapist using his – or her – hands gently or more vigorously to achieve one or more of the following aims:

- **Mobilisation** – this means freeing one or more joints in the spine, and this is accomplished by the therapist moving them, often very gently, to relieve pain or spasm.
- **Manipulation** – or realigning a joint that is or has become misplaced. Although a vigorous manoeuvre, the least force necessary is used, and this often involves a very small movement indeed.
- **Massage** – this can help relieve muscle spasm, increase circulation to the injured area and so speed up and promote the natural healing process.

Other treatment methods commonly used by physiotherapists include ice, hydrotherapy, and acupuncture. For an acute back problem, ice can reduce pain and increase circulation while hydrotherapy can help a patient move their back and limbs more freely in water than they may otherwise be able to do. The use of acupuncture for pain relief is also increasing.

OSTEOPATHY

Although still considered by many as more of an 'alternative' therapy than physiotherapy, osteopathy has nevertheless gained great acceptance from the medical profession. Developed in the late 19th century by Andrew Taylor Still, osteopathy is based on the underlying principle that 'structure governs function', and the therapy therefore relies primarily on manipulative techniques, these being mainly applied to the back and neck.

Central to the osteopathic concept is that much of the pain and disability affecting people stems from abnormalities in the function of the musculoskeletal system rather than in any identifiable or discernible pathology. According to osteopaths, impaired function in one part of the musculoskeletal system can exist without symptoms but may throw considerable strain on another part of the body.

Like physiotherapists, osteopaths build up a full picture of the patient's particular dysfunction, which may have developed over a long period of time. Says the Osteopathic Information Service: "Osteopaths do not look on patients simply as back sufferers but as individuals with their own unique requirements. Treatment is designed to correct each individual's mechanical and spinal problems in order to stimulate their own natural healing processes."

A recent survey of osteopathic practices throughout the county revealed that more than half of the patients had sought help because of low back trouble.

CHIROPRACTIC

Using treatments that are extremely similar in many ways to those employed by osteopaths, chiropractic techniques are particularly successful in treating low back pain, slipped discs and sports injuries.

A well-established health care system that originated in America, chiropractic's underlying principle is that a patient's overall state of health will be greatly governed by how comfortably and easily the various parts of his body move, naturally paying special attention to the back and the neck.

In general, chiropractors are more likely to use more vigorous techniques than osteopaths when freeing 'stuck joints' through manipulation.

ACUPUNCTURE

Based on the ages-old Oriental medical system that was first developed in China, acupuncture uses needles – or sometimes other similar objects – to stimulate specific points on the body so that this stimulation can bring about beneficial changes elsewhere in the body. One of the aims of this system is to 're-balance forces' and so improve the health of the subject as a whole as well as provide treatment for existing specific ailments.

Acupuncturists believe in the ancient Chinese philosophy that states there is a life force – called *chi* – which is made up of negative and positive flows of energy, respectively known as *yin* and *yang*, which course throughout the body along channels called meridians. Disease and pain, say the acupuncturists, are the result of an interruption or an imbalance in these flows of energy. Stimulation by acupuncture is meant to promote or re-establish the normal flow of energy along the meridians and so restore health.

Commonly used for the treatment of back pain, acupuncture has gained a considerably amount of acceptance from conventional medicine and is even used quite frequently by doctors. Although there is a great deal of dissent about how acupuncture works – one currently popular theory suggests that the needles cause the body to release additional endorphins, these being natural painkillers – there is little doubt that it certainly has been an effective treatment for sciatica and other symptoms of back problems.

If you're put off by the very idea of having needles inserted into your body, it's worth pointing out that the procedure is not in the slightest bit painful and at worst may be a touch uncomfortable. However, because it's absolutely essential that needles used during treatment be sterile, you should only consult a fully qualified practitioner.

ACUPRESSURE

This works broadly on the same principles as acupuncture, but the essential difference between the two is that in acupressure the various points on the patient's body are stimulated by the practitioner's finger or thumb instead of by the insertion of needles. One major advantage of this approach is that a patient (or a relative or friend) can perhaps be taught to perform the treatment and therefore it can be repeated as often as required at home. Most practitioners of acupuncture also offer acupressure therapy because some patients cannot face the idea of having needles stuck into them.

YOGA

This is a well-known discipline that broadly speaking consists of two separate yet closely-linked components: first, there's a series of static or stretching exercises as well as breathing exercises; secondly, there are meditation techniques that aim to help the subject attain a state of peace and harmony within the inner self.

At the physical level, yoga has proven itself to be an extremely effective way of loosening and mobilising joints whose movement has become restricted. Additionally, the meditation techniques can help reduce mental and emotional stress which can at times exacerbate back problems.

Although nearly all yoga exercises are considered to be safe for a moderately fit person, they can create a great deal of pressure on parts of the back and neck, and it's therefore essential that even the simplest of yoga exercises should only be undertaken under the supervision of a fully qualified teacher. Naturally, should you join a yoga class, make sure that the instructor is fully aware of any existing difficulties you may have.

THE ALEXANDER TECHNIQUE

As posture greatly influences how well your back works, it's not so surprising that many sufferers have found relief from their symptoms through the Alexander Technique, a training programme whose prime purpose is to overcome poor habits of posture and movement, but which also has the additional aim of reducing reaction to stress by lessening both physical and mental tension.

Training in the technique – which was devised by an Australian actor, Frederick Matthias Alexander – takes the form of a series of lessons in which the teacher guides the pupil to 'experience' their innate posture, movement and balance, which, according to Alexandrian teachings, become 'lost' or distorted by accumulated stress. Further lessons are also said to provide 'inspiration for deeper change' and bring about improvements in body-mind functioning.

FLOATATION OR 'FLOATING'

This is one of the newest weapons in the battle against back problems. Essentially, as defined by a pre-eminent scientist, floating is 'a method of attaining the deepest rest that humankind has ever experienced', and this is accomplished by spending an hour or so lying quietly in the dark, suspended in a warm solution of Epsom salts, about 10" deep, and so dense that you float without effort.

According to its proponents, floating can bring many benefits:

- In the gravity-free environment the body balances and heals internally as all the senses are rested. It is claimed that one hour of floating has the restorative effects of four hours of sleep.
- Old injuries and aches – and especially backache – experience relief as floating helps blood circulation.
- Additionally, research has shown that floating measurably reduces both blood pressure and the heart rate while at the same time also lowering the levels of stress-related chemicals in the body.

Studies having shown that during a float, people produce slower brain-waves patterns, known as the theta waves and normally experienced only during deep meditation or just before falling asleep. This is usually accompanied by vivid imagery, very clear, creative thoughts, sudden insights and inspirations or feelings of profound peace and joy, induced by the release of endorphins, the body's natural opiates.

Just how good a treatment for sciatica or other back problems floating is, still remains to be fully proven. As it's a comparatively new approach, there just aren't enough documented case histories to provide meaningful statistics. However, as it is a therapy that is unlikely to do harm and may help a lot, it may well be worth a try.

Floating, however, doesn't suit everybody as it requires a willingness on your part to let go and see what happens, and you may need to float a few times before you are able to relax completely, both physically and mentally. Incidentally, your skin won't wrinkle like a prune when you float because the water contains high salt levels and therefore doesn't rob your skin of salt, which is what causes wrinkling. Instead, floating leaves your skin soft and silky.

For details on how to find practising members of the above therapies, please see the *Appendix – Additional sources of help and information.*

CHAPTER 6

Easing the pain

While medical treatments can cure many forms of back problems, including those that give rise to sciatica, it still remains a fact that many sufferers will continue to experience pain at times because of their underlying condition. Essentially, a patient is most likely to have to cope with pain under the following circumstances:

- When the problem first manifests itself, pain being almost invariably the first symptom. Naturally, depending upon the severity of the problem, the sufferer will then either seek medical help immediately or perhaps wait a while in the hope that the symptoms ease or disappear of their own account.

- Even when medical treatment or other remedial therapy has been initiated, it may take a while for this to take full effect and pain may still be experienced now and then.

- Then, of course, many people have what might be called 'mild sciatica' in that occasionally they have pain or perhaps only discomfort, which although bothersome, they feel is not severe enough to seek medical help. It needs to be stated once again that anyone experiencing symptoms severe enough to cause concern should seek medical advice. However, there's little doubt that good though this advice is, not everyone will take it, many people preferring to try to control or reduce their pain rather than seeking to deal with the problem that may be causing it.

While the many forms of treatment available for back problems are described elsewhere in this book, in this chapter we will concentrate solely on those measures intended to eliminate or reduce pain. But first of all . . .

WHAT IS PAIN?

Something that all of us experience at times, pain is essentially a warning that your body sends to you to let you know that something is amiss. While we tend to think of the pain we feel as being the problem, it is more often merely a signal intended to draw our attention.

Demonstrating this through a fairly obvious example, you'll feel pain when you touch something that is too hot – the pain in that case causing you to withdraw your hand before further damage is done. In instances like this one, pain serves a very useful function.

Back pain and sciatica, unpleasant though they can be, also fulfil a similar purpose, in effect sending one or more of the following messages:

- You've overdone things and subjected your back to greater demands than it can cope with comfortably.
- Stop whatever it is that you're doing, it's causing harm.
- There's an underlying problem somewhere that needs attention (the message sent by sciatica is a bit confusing in this regard as it first draws attention to where the pain is felt, in the buttocks, legs, wherever, rather than to the area where the cause of it resides).
- You're being reminded that you're susceptible to back problems and you'd be well-advised to treat your spine more considerately in the future.

While pain that alerts you to a situation that needs your attention is indeed useful, there are also many instances where pain appears to be of no purpose, or at least not obviously so. Typical of this are many chronic – that is long-lasting or ongoing – pains for which there is no obvious explanation, other than perhaps that they're due to part of the nervous system failing to operate properly and as such may/could be considered as 'false alarms'.

It's also worth noting that valuable though pain is as a warning sign, its severity is by no means always directly related to the

37

seriousness of the underlying cause. For example, migraines are notorious for causing excruciating pain, yet apart from that may present little risk to overall health. On the other hand, some extremely serious diseases are marked by little or even no pain, especially in their early stages.

Although the severity of sciatica and other pain symptoms related to back problems are usually a fairly good indication of how bad the problem is at that moment, it isn't always so. Many factors influence how strongly a given individual perceives and reacts to pain, so it's perfectly possible that two patients with back problems of equal severity may experience widely varying degrees of pain.

DEALING WITH PAIN

For relatively mild pain, the cause of which is known or strongly suspected, the usual first line of defence (apart from rest and seeking advice) consists of taking analgesics, that is drugs that relieve pain. These medications can be divided in two broad groups:

- 'Mild' analgesics, such as aspirin, ibuprofen, paracetamol and similar preparations, that can be bought over the counter without a prescription; and
- More potent analgesics, including narcotic analgesics such as morphine and pethidine, which have to be prescribed by a doctor.

While the dosage of any prescribed medication will of course be determined by your doctor, there are some points you should keep in mind when self-medicating with mild analgesics:

- All drugs – including even aspirin, that standard standby found in almost every household – have potential side-effects, although they're usually safe when used correctly.
- Many medications also become less and less effective the longer and more frequently you use them. Additionally, the effect of many analgesics is not necessarily increased pro rata by larger dosages which do, however, normally bring a greater risk of side-effects.

- Some kinds of pain, particularly those resulting from nerve damage, may not respond or only slightly so to simple analgesics. If your pain is not eased by ordinary painkillers, then that is an obvious indication that professional help should be sought.

PRESCRIBED MEDICATIONS

Should your pain fail to respond sufficiently to mild analgesics, your doctor can choose from a wide variety of more potent remedies, those commonly used in treating back problems including codeine-based drugs, narcotic drugs, and non-steroidal anti-inflammatories. Additionally, epidural injections have been used, but this approach still remains somewhat controversial.

Should the pain persist at an unacceptable level, your doctor or consultant may refer you to a specialist Pain Clinic for assessment and possible management of the pain, and for help in living a fuller life in spite of the pain.

PAIN MANAGEMENT CLINICS

Not all hospitals have these special clinics that usually include teams of doctors, psychologists, nurses, physiotherapists, occupational therapists and others who together run 'pain management programmes' that aim to teach patients about pain, how best to cope with it and how to live a more active life. Acupuncture and other complementary therapies may be available through some of these clinics. Explaining the role of pain clinics, *The Pain Society* stated: "Pain management helps sufferers come to terms with what has happened to their lives and to accept that they may not find a magic answer to cure their pain. Unfortunately, there are times when no treatment for chronic pain works as well as we would like. The pain sufferer is then left with a difficult problem of continuing pain, and all the negative effects the pain can have on every part of life, including work, marriage, social life, mobility, mood and sleep. The 'ripples' of pain are not the same as the pain itself, but often go with it and make the whole experience much more difficult to cope with, both for the pain sufferer and for those close to them."

OTHER PAIN MANAGEMENT TECHNIQUES

Two lesser known but at times extremely successful methods of easing pain also worth considering are:

Transcutaneous Electrical Nerve Stimulation (TENS). This method works somewhat on the same principle that makes pain diminish when you rub an injured area. However, instead of rubbing the painful spot, the TENS unit – a small battery-powered electronic unit you can clip to your belt or carry in a pocket – sends small electrical impulses to conductive pads placed near where it hurts. The electrical impulses are transmitted through the pads to the local nerve endings and reduce the capacity of the nerves to transmit pain signals to the receptors in the brain, so effectively reducing your perception of the pain. Note, however, that although TENS treatment can lessen pain it does not cure the underlying condition responsible for it.

While TENS units are potentially available for loan to suitable patients under the NHS, they are usually in very short supply. You can, however, also buy a unit yourself (no prescription is needed) and one well-established supplier of these is *Dezac Ltd*, 54 Bath Road, Cheltenham, Glos GL53 7HG (Tel: 01242 583502), whose Rio TENS unit offers both variable intensity control and six different treatment programmes.

ELECTROMAGNETIC THERAPY

Using magnetic sources to influence the body's state of health is, of course, not a new idea, but what is new is that today's ever more sensitive electronic instruments can now track down and confirm the various effects. From this modern research into an ages-old therapy has emerged confirmation that some types of pain can be reduced by the application of magnets.

Just how magnetic therapy works is still a matter of some controversy and needs much further study. The most likely explanation is the one put forward by physicist and psychologist Dr Buryl Payne, a scientist who is the inventor of the first biofeedback instruments and former professor at Boston University and Goddard College, and who has made a lifelong study of magnetic therapy. He says that two specific factors now known to be involved in magnetic therapy are:

- The promotion of increased blood flow with resultant increased oxygen-carrying capacity, both of which can help combat pain by assisting the body's natural ability to heal itself.
- The induction of changes in the migration of calcium ions which can help move calcium away from painful, arthritic joints, thereby reducing the accompanying symptomatic pain.

The use of magnetic therapy to control pain is usually applied through placing simple magnets directly upon the area of pain. They can either be used for brief periods or else taped into place for ongoing treatment. Information about self-therapy can be obtained from manuals or from a qualified practitioner. Alternatively, devices that emit much stronger magnetic fields, usually in a 'pulsed' form, are used by qualified therapists.

Apart from aiding in pain reduction, magnetic therapy has also been used to good effect to reinforce and improve spinal alignment, assisting the vertebrae of the spine to align properly, both vertically and laterally. Major successes have been obtained in patients suffering from sciatica.

THE FOOD CONNECTION

Apart from the methods outlined above, you may also be able to lessen the extent to which you feel pain by making changes in your diet, as modern medical research has underlined the long-known fact that some foods have properties that can reduce how strongly you perceive pain.

Here are some recent key findings:

Extremely promising results have been obtained with a diet specifically formulated to reduce many forms of chronic pain, including those resulting from back problems and joint dysfunction. Dr Samuel Selzer, of Temple University in Philadelphia, who headed the group that developed the special diet, however, warned: "Although this diet has brought great relief to many who followed it and it is safe for most people, you should always consult your doctor before you try it." The pain-relieving diet consists of several components:

1) Increase your intake of complex carbohydrates – such as whole-grain foods (but excluding corn), beans, vegetables, and fruit – so that these account for about three quarters of your food intake; and

2) Avoid all fats and oils, including butter and margarine, as much as possible; and

3) Also avoid refined carbohydrates, including sugar, honey, and syrup; and

4) Keep as low as possible your consumption of processed or baked foods that contain a great deal of fats, oils, or sugar; and

5) While following the guidelines above, you should take three grams of tryptophan, an amino acid normally available from health foods stores, daily, dividing the total amount into six equal doses of half a gram each, one of these being taken at about three-hourly intervals. Tryptophan is converted by the body into serotonin, a natural pain-relieving chemical.

6) Follow the diet rigorously for at least four weeks. If after that time it has brought benefits and there has been less pain, then reduce the tryptophan to a total of only two grams daily. Assess the results again a month later; if progress continues, once again cut down on the tryptophan, this time to only half a gram a day.

Instead of taking tryptophan supplements, you can follow the diet above without the tryptophan, but make up for this by substantially increasing your intake of foods with a high tryptophan to protein ratio, these including soya beans, dairy products, fish, meat, and eggs.

Other food-related suggestions for combating pain:

- The effect of aspirin will be accelerated if you drink a cup of strong coffee at the same time, according to research conducted by Dr Bernard Schachel of Yale University.
- Eating chilli peppers can help reduce pain because they are an excellent source of capsaicin, a substance found by researchers at the University of Alabama to diminish many kinds of pain, especially chronic pains, including those associated with pinched nerves as in sciatica.
- Easily available foods with proven pain-reducing properties include cloves, garlic, ginger, onions, and peppermint.
- Many plant foods have a high content of salicylates, a sort of natural aspirin that has analgesic effects and can also combat inflammation. Good sources of this natural painkiller include cherries, prunes, blueberries, curry powder, dried currants and dates, paprika, and liquorice.

CHAPTER 7

Tips to prevent back pain and sciatica

As with every other ailment, it is naturally better to prevent back pain and sciatica from arising in the first place than having to cope with it afterwards.

Protecting your back from unnecessary or avoidable strain or stress is an important part of overcoming any existing problems as well as preventing possible future ones. Taking sensible precautions will help you cope with your condition in three key ways:

1) The first and most obvious benefit is that just treating your back more kindly may be enough by itself to stop the back pain or sciatica altogether.

2) Even when precautionary measures fail to relieve your symptoms totally, these will almost certainly be greatly eased.

3) And, perhaps most important of all, protecting your back may stop further damage from taking place.

Setting aside difficulties arising from injury, accident or disease, back problems arise in general because one of two scenarios, or a combination of these:

- A specific event during which you put your back under greater strain than it can cope, without something giving way – this could be lifting something that was just too heavy for you, or bending down awkwardly, or even perhaps just spending a long time sitting or working in a position that placed extra strain on your back.

- An ongoing sequence of events that gradually strained your back, none of these events being harmful enough to cause serious trouble by themselves, but their cumulative effect eventually adding up to a back that's become troublesome.

Although at first glance it might appear from the above that precautionary measures to protect your back could be divided into two main groups – those aimed at preventing specific events harming you and those that deal with more general precautions – it's not that easy to classify them that way because they often overlap to a great extent. For example, while it's obvious that everyone – even people with no signs of back problems – should be careful and sensible when lifting or picking up anything heavy, this is advice that should be followed at all times, not merely when you think the item you're lifting is particularly heavy, or when you think your back is getting ready to 'play up' once again. It's a fact that it's just as possible to strain your back badly when lifting something comparatively light, but doing this incorrectly, than when picking up something heavier.

But it's not just lifting that puts your back at risk. Says the Osteopathic Information Service: "Many other common activities such as ironing, vacuuming, gardening, making a bed, and driving a car, if carried out incorrectly, can also lead to problems.

"Lifting, however, is particularly hazardous. Most people know the theory but forget to apply it in the heat of the moment. Remember: stand as close as you can; bend at the knees and keep your back straight; try to avoid lifting and twisting at the same time; get some help if you need to lift a heavy piece of furniture. Similarly, it should be a case of all things in moderation when you are stretching. Stand on a firm chair or ladder rather than stretching too far to dust or paint the ceiling and, conversely, kneel rather than bend down to reach low shelves or dust the skirting-boards.

"For many energetic activities – and housework or gardening can fall into this category if you approach them enthusiastically – it is best to work up gradually. Tackle lighter jobs first to warm up and loosen the joints before taking on more demanding bending and stretching tasks.

"As a general rule, use smooth, controlled movements rather than jerky ones and, if you do feel pain at any time, stop. Avoid the temptation to do 'just that last little bit'. Pain is a vital warning sign and should not be ignored."

However, it's not just when you're active that your back may be at risk. Poor posture or bad seating can equally contribute to making your problems all the worse. And your bed, of course, plays a vital role in keeping you and your spine rested (for more information about sleeping arrangements, see *Chapter 9 – Better quality sleep to ease and prevent back trouble*).

GOOD POSTURE – THE KEY TO A LESS TROUBLESOME BACK

Posture – that is how the various parts of your body are positioned at a given time – will greatly affect how much pressure is exerted upon your spine as well as, perhaps more importantly, *how* that pressure is exerted. As we've seen, the spine is at best a somewhat unstable structure whose design is such that it takes relatively little of the wrong kind of pressure to set off back pain. The 'building-blocks' that make up the spine will be at their most effective and stable in carrying the weight of the upper body when your back is relatively straight, as well as supported correctly whenever support is possible or available. Translating these general principles into specific recommendations, you'll reduce the demands placed upon your spine by following these guide-lines:

- When walking, try to maintain as upright a posture as possible, keeping your shoulders reasonably far back rather than allowing them to drop forwards. Keep your head up straight – as though it were suspended from an imaginary 'sky hook'.
- Also, seek to maintain an upright posture when standing still. However, if you have to stand still for any length of time, do try to move somewhat, even if it's only a few steps, at frequent intervals. Not only will this make it easier for you to stand upright

and avoid slouching, it will also help the blood circulate better to your legs and lower body.

■ When seated, make sure that the chair you're using gives good support for the small of your back and also is of the correct height for you. Heavily-padded 'soft' chairs you sink into are usually bad news for your back as is half-lying, half-sitting on a sofa or large easy chair. Once again, try to keep your spine and head as upright as possible.

Other excellent recommendations to reduce the risk of back and muscle trouble are to be found in *Muscles Matter*, a booklet published by DDD/Dendron Ltd, the makers of Ibuleve, from which many of these tips for members of groups especially at risk have been extracted.

GARDENING PITFALLS

Doctors always know when spring has sprung. They start getting visits from gardeners – both young and old – who, getting back to work in the garden after the winter, have damaged their muscles.

The difficulties arise not just because of the sudden onset of activity in the cold and damp – but also because of the many opportunities that gardening offers for overstretching, bending too far for too long and lifting heavy loads.

Following these suggestions will help reduce the risk:

■ Before you start, stretch your muscles with a gentle warm-up.

■ Wear loose clothes and sturdy shoes or boots.

■ Choose your equipment carefully: lightweight, long-handled tools mean you don't have to stretch arms and legs to the limit. Hover-mowers need particular care – don't swing them around from your waist and keep as upright as possible, with the handle close to your body.

■ Overenthusiastic digging and weeding often cause damage. Don't take huge spadefuls when you're digging and keep your back as straight as you can. When weeding, kneel down as close as you can to the bed. If you're pulling out a deep-rooted plant, take the strain on your arms and legs, not your back.

Some additional tips for gardeners from Dr Arthur Grayzel, senior vice-president for medical affairs of the Arthritis Foundation in America. He suggests:

- Some people will feel more comfortable by not kneeling on the ground, but instead sitting on a small stool, so further reducing stress on the joints.
- Use plant containers that are high off the ground – or small raised garden beds – to reduce stretching and bending.
- Don't work for long periods with a tool that you have to grasp firmly.
- Divide your garden in several smaller areas and concentrate on one of these at a time to avoid overdoing things.
- Don't grip heavy loads with your fingers or arms, but *carry* them in your arms.
- Look in your garden centre for tools specially made for people with arthritis – even if you're not affected by this disease – as equipment designed for the arthritic will also often help prevent back strain.

DO-IT-YOURSELF ENTHUSIASTS

Before tackling even the simplest of DIY jobs, make sure you have the right equipment. Balancing on a chair, rather than a ladder, for example, puts undue stress on the back. Wear comfortable, loose-fitting clothes which don't restrict mobility. Also consider muscle-savers such as long-handled paint rollers. Try to have all your equipment conveniently to hand so you're not twisting and straining to reach for it.

There are always going to be some tasks which you can't avoid and which you know will put you at risk of back pain – painting the ceiling, for example. In these instances, take regular breaks and gently stretch your arms and neck at frequent intervals to reduce the risk.

OFFICE WORKERS

Spending 40 or more hours a week sitting down and using equipment that demands repetitive actions can lead to stresses and strains, from continual backache to one of the relatively recently identified repetitive strain injuries.

A good sitting position is vital. Your feet should be flat on the floor (or on a footstool) and your back reasonably straight. If the seat is adjustable, tilting it forward a little may prove more comfortable and can encourage better posture. If the seat isn't adjustable and the lower back is not supported, roll up a towel or use a small cushion for support. Pull the chair close to the desk to avoid leaning forward and putting strain on your back.

Any equipment you use frequently throughout the day such as files, the telephone and computer, should be easy to reach without overstretching. Constant use of the telephone – particularly if it's cradled between the ear and shoulder – can result in tension to the neck and shoulder area.

Try to do a number of different work activities during your day, varying your posture every so often to stretch your back and relax your muscles.

MOTHERS WITH YOUNG CHILDREN

The one thing mothers of babies and toddlers do more than just about anyone else is bend – to lift baby into the car or put them on their hip, or to tidy up toys or just picking up baby for a cuddle.

Bending can create a greater stress on the spine than almost any other movement – so it's important to do it right. Squat down rather than bend to pick things off the floor – including your child. Use the muscles in your legs and arms to lift – they're stronger than those in the back.

Other tips to reduce strain when bending:
- Kneel down by the bath when bathing children.
- Always lower the side of the cot when attending to a child.

49

- Make sure the baby's changing mat is on a surface that is at the right height to prevent overstretching the back muscles.

It's only natural to act quickly in response to a crying or bored child. But moving rapidly to prevent tears can mean creating hazardous demands on your back – such as those resulting from twisting, overstretching, or lifting loads badly – which will slow you down in the long run.

SPORTS PEOPLE

Sports injuries are mainly caused by contact with another person, an object, or through overuse of muscles. Obviously, not all such risks can be avoided – you can't foresee a collision on the pitch or a fall on the track – but they can be minimised.

Getting the body ready for exercise is just as important whether you play sport every day or once a month. It's particularly important for older people and those not used to exercising. If you are unused to exercise, a visit to your doctor before you start is always a good idea. Gently warm up for five to ten minutes to improve muscle flexibility. Before going on an energetic sporting holiday, such as skiing, start your exercise programme about six weeks beforehand. It's also important to ease your body back down after activity, first with mild physical exercise, then gentle stretching exercises to help prevent muscle stiffness. Changing into warm clothing stops the body getting chilled.

Clothes and equipment should be chosen with care: shoes must fit properly and be correct for the purpose; clothes should be appropriate, and your racket, bike or clubs should be of the right size for your height and weight.

HOME WORKERS

Bending over beds, heaving a vacuum cleaner around, dusting in corners and standing cooking in the kitchen are all ingredients that add up to a recipe for increased risk of back strain and other muscle pain.

It's easy to mistreat your body as you give the carpet a clean – twisting from the waist to get the vacuum cleaner into position can harm the back and strain the arms. Keep the handle close to your body and use the machine's wheels to move it around.

Beds are usually designed for the benefit of the sleeper, not the one who has to change the sheets. To make changing bed linen safer, don't lean over to the other side to tuck sheets in, but go round to do it. Similarly, pictures are designed to be looked at, not cleaned; floors to be trodden on, not bent down to for cleaning. But a long-handled duster and brooms used with an upright back, with the handle held close to the body, will help you avoid strains.

The height of work surfaces such as ironing-boards and kitchen units is also important to avoid uncomfortable bending. The most efficient height is usually 2-4 inches below elbow height. In fact, ironing is often best done sitting down, with the chair close to the board.

DRIVING

Many car seats are truly badly designed and that is why people who drive a lot are much more likely to have back problems. For example, those who spend more than half of their working day driving are three times more likely to suffer a slipped disc, says Mark Porter, of Loughborough University, who has made a special study of the subject. "And these people also have a 16 per cent higher incidence of lower back pain," he added.

Tips to make driving kinder to your back:

- Make certain that your driving seat provides good support. If it doesn't, you can probably improve this by judiciously placing small cushions – or rolled up towelling – where the extra support is needed.
- Ensure that you have enough room to extend your legs comfortably while your feet retain good contact with accelerator, brake and clutch pedals.

- Whenever possible, break a long journey into several shorter ones. Stop every hour or so.
- Make certain that all driving mirrors and all other adjustable controls are in their correct positions so that you can use these comfortably without stretching and straining your neck and spine.

SPECIALLY FOR COMPUTER USERS

Anyone using a computer is all too likely to spend long hours typing away in one position, perhaps also leaning forward to see the screen more clearly as well as reaching out to move the mouse over its mat, all activities that can lead to back trouble if they're not performed with due care.

An excellent set of guidelines to prevent problems arising from the prolonged use of a computer has been produced by the Osteopathic Information Service. Although these tips were initially formulated especially for young people, they are equally relevant to members of all age groups. This is what the Osteopathic Information Service recommends:

- How you sit in front of a computer is important: your spine needs to be straight and your forearms should be horizontal in front of you, with your hands resting lightly on the keyboard.
- Your feet should rest on the floor.
- The monitor screen should be directly in front of you (not off-set) and the top of it should be level with your eyeline (an imaginary line drawn from your eyes to the top of the monitor). The screen should not be too near or too far (25 inches or 640mm should be about right).
- You may find these basic requirements difficult to meet in full. For instance, if you are not very tall, your chair may be too high for you to rest your feet on the floor. If this is the case, use a footrest of suitable height, either buying one or making your own by taping together several old telephone directories.
- Reflections on your screen may cause you to adopt an awkward

52

posture. Try not to face a window or sit with your back to one; sitting sideways to a window is best. Ceiling lighting may also give trouble: get a desk light and turn off ceiling or suspended lights, if possible.

▪ Most important of all is the length of time you spend in a static posture. Get up after half an hour and have a good stretch for five minutes or so. Walk around and shake out your arms and hands. If possible try to vary the work you are doing.

This check-list will help you remember the points made above:

1) Sit straight – use backrest of chair.
2) Rest feet on the floor – use a footstool if necessary.
3) Forearms horizontal in front of you.
4) Screen directly in front of you – not to one side.
5) Top of screen level with your eyeline.
6) Screen approximately 25 inches (640mm) away from you.
7) Use a desk light if possible.
8) Desk sideways to daylight if possible.
9) Stand up and stretch for five minutes in every half hour.
10) Try to plan some variation in your work.

CHAPTER 8

Lightening the burden

It stands to reason that being at all overweight is not going to help your sciatica or back problems one bit. As we've seen, the spine's design is such that it all too often has difficulty in coping with even the normal, ordinary demands put upon it through everyday living. If the burden it has to bear becomes even greater because you're overweight, then it's obviously more likely that something is going to give sooner or later.

There's an additional point to take into account: most overweight people carry their extra pounds in the abdomen area, the hips and the thighs. Extra weight in the abdomen is particularly bad news for back sufferers because its presence not only puts extra strain upon the spine while you're erect – such as standing or walking – but even when you're sitting. And, of course, bending over or lifting anything creates even greater demands upon the spine when there's excess baggage hanging out in front of it.

Keeping your weight down to a reasonable level can make a major difference in both preventing and easing back problems and sciatica. What's more, of course, keeping to a healthy weight will also pay rich dividends in other health benefits. Additionally, many of the exercises that are so important to maintaining a flexible and trouble-free spine will be a great deal easier to do if you're not carrying too many extra pounds– and a lot more fun, too! It's a fact that the overweight – the very people who would perhaps gain the greatest benefits from frequent and regular exercising – are often those who exercise the least, part of the reason for this obviously being that exercising is all that much harder and therefore less appealing for them. This lack of exercising often imposes a double penalty upon the back: firstly, it is likely to contribute to the putting on of ever more extra weight; secondly, because the back muscles are not exercised, they're likely to be in poor condition, lacking strength and flexibility, providing less efficient support for the back and the spine as a whole.

Faced with an obese patient with recurrent sciatica or other back problems for which no other obvious treatment is indicated, doctors will often recommend a weight-loss programme. Good though that advice is, most doctors unfortunately do not have the time to provide specific guidelines about how best to shed the pounds. Following are some of the things your doctor might suggest if he had the time.

ARE YOU OVERWEIGHT?

Most overweight people are pretty well aware of the fact that they should lose weight, but many are not quite sure about the extent of the problem they face. To find out where you stand, compare your weight to that listed for someone of your height and sex in the following table to get a pretty accurate idea of what your weight should be – and from that you can then easily calculate how many pounds, if any, you should aim to lose.

Height (feet, inches)	Range of acceptable weights (in pounds)	
	Men	Women
4'10"		92 – 119
4'11"		94 – 122
5'0"		96 – 125
5'1"		99 – 128
5'2"	112 – 141	102 – 131
5'3"	115 – 144	105 – 134
5'4"	118 – 148	108 – 138
5'5"	121 – 152	111 – 142
5'6"	124 – 156	114 – 146

Height (feet, inches)	Range of acceptable weights (in pounds) Men	Women
5'7"	128 – 161	118 – 150
5'8"	132 – 166	122 – 154
5'9"	136 – 170	126 – 158
5'10"	140 – 174	130 – 163
5'11"	144 – 179	134 – 168
6'0"	148 – 184	138 – 173
6'1"	152 – 189	
6'2"	156 – 194	
6'3"	160 – 199	
6'4"	164 – 204	

Please note that when using this table, the height is that without wearing shoes and the weight is that without clothes. To convert the above figures into metric measurements: 1 foot equals about 0.3 metres; 1 pound equals about 0.45 kilograms.

As you will have seen, the range covered by each set of figures is quite broad, encompassing a difference from 27 to 40 pounds. The reason for this quite wide variance is that there simply is no *exact* weight that someone of a given height and sex should be ideally. Many other factors also play a major role in determining what is right and healthy for any given individual, such as the kind of build you have, whether you're relatively thin- or thick-boned, and also, of course, to a large extent, your age. Nevertheless, these figures provide a pretty good guide, and if your weight is near the top end for your range, then it's sensible to make sure that you don't put on any more pounds. Because you're someone with a very specific problem – that of lower back pain and/or sciatica – you should aim at bringing your weight down so that you end up at the lower rather than the upper end of the range.

By the way, it should be noted that there is quite a difference between being merely somewhat overweight and being obese, despite the fact that the two terms are generally used somewhat interchangeably. From a medical point of view, you're only considered obese if you're at least 20 per cent heavier than your recommended weight. Of course, if your weight problem is such that you are truly obese, then it's even all the more important that you start losing the pounds.

WEIGHT GAIN OR LOSS? IT'S A SIMPLE EQUATION

Apart from the relatively few cases where obesity is caused by a hormonal disorder, most instances of being overweight are simply the result of eating more food than is required to produce the calories needed by the body to sustain its requirements, the excess intake then gradually accumulating in the body, mainly in the subcutaneous tissues.

If eating more than your body needs brings on weight gain, then it follows from this that the only way either to prevent becoming overweight or losing weight if you already weight too much is the reverse: follow a diet that provides everything your body needs, but no more than that. While exercising, because it makes you burn up extra calories, can make a useful contribution to any weight-losing programme, this is not likely to have a substantial enough effect to really bring down your weight to any great extent. The bottom line – no pun intended – for achieving worthwhile weight loss is regularly to eat fewer calories than your normal daily requirements. There are, of course, hundreds of different diet plans, but the only ones that can succeed are those which cause you to eat fewer calories than your body consumes. Just how many calories someone needs varies considerably, but as a rule of thumb most otherwise healthy people following relatively sedentary occupations will begin to start losing weight when their average daily intake falls below 1,500 calories.

Like so much other good advice, that about eating less is obviously a good deal easier to offer than to follow. The suggestions that follow can, however, help you devise your own slimming plan, one that best suits your own circumstances and therefore places the fewest demands upon you.

First, some general guidelines:

- Do not be overambitious when planning your diet by seeking to lose a great deal of weight in a short period of time. It's far better to lose only a pound or two a week and to be able to comfortably maintain this rate of loss than it is to try for much greater weight loss and fail because the diet is too demanding. Remember, it took years – possibly decades – for you to become overweight, so don't expect this to be remedied overnight. A little patience can be rewarding.

- Eat your meals at regular times and stick to that routine. Snacking is probably the slimmer's greatest enemy.

- Within the calories you allow yourself daily, try to have as many of these as possible from food that's solid rather than liquid. Solid food is more satisfying inwardly, and so will increase the length of time before you feel hungry again, thereby aiding you in keeping your calorie intake down.

- Foods that contain a good deal of dietary fibre are usually more 'filling', meaning that a smaller amount of them satisfies hunger better. Studies have shown that eating more high-fibre foods can be an extremely effective way to bring about sustainable weight loss. Typical foods high in fibre include vegetables, fruit, and wholegrain cereals.

- Calories provided by food come from three basic sources: carbohydrates, proteins, and fats. On average, a given weight of fat will contain more than twice the calories found in an equal weight of carbohydrates or proteins – which means that one of the most obvious and sensible ways to cut your calorie intake is by reducing your consumption of foods with a high fat content.

- Women starting out on a slimming diet will probably find it easier to stick to it if they begin it during the first two weeks of their menstrual cycle. At this time their oestrogen level will be high and this hormone has an appetite-curbing effect.

Some specific recommendations:

- Sugar, of course, is very high in calories, and foods containing a good deal of it should be avoided. What's more, researchers have discovered that table sugar, apart from its calories, can have a second undesirable effect upon would-be slimmers in that it can stimulate them into increasing their overall calorie consumption.
- Alcohol is also high in calories, so best avoided altogether or only consumed extremely moderately.
- Whole milk is high in fat – a pint of it contains 22 grams of fat. Use skimmed milk which has only half a gram of fat per pint.
- Chicken and turkey are both low in fat, providing the skin is removed first. Stripping away the skin removes most of the fat because it is mainly found directly underneath it and will easily come away as the skin is lifted.

MORE TIPS TO TRY

There are also numerous 'tricks', psychological or otherwise, that you can use to good effect to help you feel less hungry or make a smaller portion of food just as satisfying as a larger one. Researchers have found that the following ideas work well for most people, enabling them to adhere more easily to a restricted diet:

- Drink a full glass of water half an hour or so before every main meal. The water makes you feel fuller when you begin to eat, so reducing your appetite.
- Serve your food on plates smaller than those you normally use. The smaller plate will make a slimmer's portion appear bigger than it really is, so deceiving your brain into believing that you're having a larger meal than you are. Extending the same principle, try eating with a cocktail fork. This will force you into eating more slowly – the more slowly you eat, the more filling the food will seem to be.
- Another useful 'psychological' tip in the same vein is to select food that is low in calories but which takes up a lot of room on

your plate. Studies have shown that we eat what looks like the amount of food we think we want, subconsciously judging portions by the space they occupy. This means that choosing low-calorie foods, such as salads, that fill a lot of space on your plate can provide you with the illusion that you're eating more.

- Perhaps a rather extreme tip, but one that he swears is truly most effective, comes from an American slimming expert who suggests that you can make yourself eat less by making your food look unattractive by shining a green light on it.

Some more eminently practical suggestions that you can use to train yourself to eat less:

- Much as you may hate to throw away good food, do not save leftovers from meals. Stashing away leftovers in the fridge, say the experts, is unconscious plotting to provide yourself with snacks between meals.

- Keep foods that are low in calories in easily accessible places in your cupboards or fridge while placing high-calorie foods where they're difficult to get to.

- In so far as this is practicable, eat alone instead of in the company of others. Studies have determined that people eating on their own consume fewer calories on the average than those having a meal as part of a group. Additionally, those eating alone also spent less time at the table, thereby reducing the length of time during which they could have been tempted into having an extra helping.

SUMMING IT UP

Losing weight can be a very good way to reduce the severity and frequency of symptoms of back pain. And, of course, another great virtue of this approach is that it will also automatically bring many other major health benefits.

CHAPTER 9

Better quality sleep to ease and prevent back trouble

How well you sleep and what kind of bed you sleep on can affect your sciatica or back pain in several important ways:

1) As we've already seen, posture affects the spine – and that also applies to the posture you adopt when you're in bed. It stands to reason that lying for hours on end in a bed with a sagging mattress that provides poor support and forces your spine, legs and neck to adopt uncomfortable positions is simply not going to make back pain or sciatica any the better.

2) A good restful night's sleep is one of Nature's greatest healers. Equally, tossing and turning all night is a sure-fire recipe for waking up the next morning feeling worse than when you went to bed, with a stiff, aching spine and your back muscles all knotted up.

3) The average adult grows in the night by as much as two centimetres. During the day the spine gradually becomes more and more compressed as the cumulative effect of gravity takes its toll. At night, as we lay down and the weight of our upper body no longer presses downward, the spine is given a chance to straighten and recover. Just how much straightening out and recovery takes place during sleep will be greatly affected by how suitable your bed is.

Confirmation of the importance that their sleeping arrangements hold for back pain sufferers was evidenced by a recent survey that discovered that 93 per cent of general practitioners interviewed agreed that a good new bed can help alleviate back problems. While this survey was admittedly carried out on behalf of a group of bed manufacturers with a vested interest in promoting the sale of their products, the essential message that emerges still remains true: the right kind of bed (although not necessarily a new one) can work wonders for anyone suffering from sciatica or other back problems.

Naturally, just as important as your choice of bed is how you sleep in it. Let us look at these two separate but interlinked questions one at a time, beginning with . . .

WHAT KIND OF BED IS BEST?

Although the above seems like a simple enough question that should evoke an equally simple answer, the truth is that, as is so often the case, experts do have widely differing views. What's more, what is a good and comfortable bed for one person is not necessarily so for the next, as what suits best does vary greatly from individual to individual. To take two extreme examples, even today many Japanese still sleep on traditional *futons*, thin strips of flock-filled bedding which are unrolled on the floor at bedtime, while there is a great vogue for waterbeds in many other parts of the world. The contrast between the two sleeping arrangements could hardly be greater – ranging from the sleeper being almost directly in contact with the hard floor to lolling about in the deep moving trough of a waterbed. Yet both methods have their keen proponents who would argue strongly the merits of their choice. The truth is that neither sleeping arrangement is *per se* the right one – the fact that both are acceptable for many people just shows that the human body can adapt to and accept a wide range of sleeping conditions.

Even in Britain, where the overwhelming majority of people favour what might be called 'ordinary' beds consisting of a base and mattress, there is wide variation in what people find comfortable. Experts, however, agree that to play its part in easing or preventing back pain or sciatica, your bed should meet the following criteria:

- It must provide 'good' support for the whole body and so prevent the spine from sagging.
- It must be of a height that makes it easy to get into and out of bed. The height is also of importance when it comes to making the bed or changing bedding – a low bed means there will be more bending over than with a comparatively high one.
- It must be large enough to allow plenty of room for movement during the night. Naturally, if you share your bed it should then be big enough to provide adequate space for two.

Let us now look at these key points in greater detail.

GOOD SUPPORT

There's a general belief that if you have back problems, then your bed should be as hard as possible, even to the extent of sleeping on a hard board rather than a mattress. That belief is a dangerous fallacy because a bed that's too hard can be just as bad for your back as one that's too soft.

Says *The National Back Pain Association* (NBPA): "We do not recommend rock-hard mattresses for bad backs. The term 'orthopaedic' has misled people into buying ultra hard beds in the hope of finding relief. Far from easing a back problem, an impossibly hard bed could simply make the condition more uncomfortable than ever. On the other hand, a bed which is too soft can inhibit ease of movement and makes the spine sag, stretching and straining the ligaments that support it."

The NBPA suggests a simple test to assess whether your bed provides the correct support. This is what you do:

- Lie down on the bed (preferably wearing only very thin clothing or none at all) and slide one of your hands, palm down, between the small of your back and the mattress.
- Now ask yourself how easy it was to insert your hand between your back and the mattress. If you had to struggle to push your hand through, then the bed is probably too soft. If your hand

slipped in so easily that there was quite a gap between it and the two surfaces, then the bed is probably too hard. However, if your hand slid through fairly easily but without there being a large gap, then the support provided is just about right.

Simple though this test is, it is nevertheless a remarkably good guide as it takes into account the two major variables that determine whether the support is correct: the firmness of the mattress and the weight of the sleeper. Naturally, if you share your bed, then this test should be carried out by both of you at the same time.

There are two inexpensive ways to 'cure' a bed that's too soft to provide adequate support:

- The simplest and least intrusive solution is to place a board between the mattress and the top of the bed's base. While almost anything that's solid and big enough can be used as a bed-board, it's really best to have one made from plywood or blockboard that's cut to the right size. Alternatively, you can buy bed-boards – including some that fold away – from specialist suppliers (see the *Appendix*).

- Another possibility is to place your mattress directly on the floor. Of course, one drawback to this approach is that it will mean that your bed will be very low indeed and you may experience considerable difficulty getting in and out of it. Making it won't be good for your back, either!

Do keep in mind that the methods above will only make a difference if your bed has a sprung base – if you have one with a solid base, that will already be as hard as it can be, and all that's left in that case is to change the mattress for a firmer one.

A bed that's too hard is more difficult to improve and it may be best to think about replacing it. In the meantime, you may find that placing a foam or fibre-filled overlay on the mattress can help.

THE CORRECT HEIGHT

The height of your bed from the floor is another major factor that should be taken into account. The NBPA suggests that you should ask yourself two questions, both about your present bed and when considering buying a new one:

1) Can you get off and on the bed easily?
2) Is the bed of a height that will be comfortable for making each day and changing bedding?

If your bed is too low but otherwise perfectly okay, there's no need to buy a new one as you usually can make it higher either by buying special extensions for its legs or, if it has legs that screw in, replacing these with longer ones. However, be sure that whatever you do will be solid enough to take the weight safely. For example, just placing a bed's four legs on blocks of wood could mean that one of the legs may slip off eventually, perhaps making the bed suddenly tilt sharply while you're asleep.

A bed that's too high can be lowered by sawing its feet. Do be absolutely sure, however, that the resulting height will be the right one for you as cutting an inch or two off the legs is one thing, gluing the pieces back, quite another!

BIG ENOUGH FOR COMFORT

A bed that's too small is obviously not going to promote a good night's sleep nor help provide your spine with the rest it needs to recuperate as much as possible from the previous day's exertions.

When considering the size of your bed, take the following into account:

- People don't just lie in one position all night, but instead are almost continuously on the move. Research has shown that during a night's sleep, most people toss and turn as many as 60 or 70 times – and your bed has to be large enough to allow for these movements without you ending up partly out of it.
- On the average, we are now both taller and heavier than we were, the UK population having grown upwards and outwards in the past 30 years. Women have gained an extra 1.05kg (more than

two pounds) in weight and 1.75cm (more than half an inch) in height. Men have put on an extra 3cms (more than an inch) in height. As we have changed, so have our bed requirements. While these increases seem minimal, they are nevertheless large enough to spell the difference between a bed that's barely big enough and one that's just too small for comfort.

The NBPA offers this advice: "A standard 4'6" double bed only gives each person 2'3" of space to sleep in – no more than a baby has in a cot! If you do suffer from a back problem, a squeezed and cramped night's sleep on a bed that rates amongst the smallest standard size in Europe will not help."

WHAT SLEEPING POSITIONS ARE BEST?

This is another one of those seemingly simple questions for which there's no simple answer, especially when you consider that no matter what position you choose as you drift into sleep is not going to be maintained throughout the night as you move about.

However, while you have relatively little control over what positions your body will adopt of its own volition while you're asleep, there are some things you can do that will help ensure that your back is going to derive the maximum benefit from your night's rest. Here are some suggestions from the NBPA and other experts:

- A good supportive pillow is important. Remember, that the main purpose of a pillow is to provide support for the neck rather than the head, and ideally your pillow should be such that it helps keep the neck vertebrae in a straight line with the vertebrae of the back. While most people do need a pillow, one that is too thick or too many of them can provoke neck pain.

- Back pain sufferers may find that lying on their side with a thin pillow or a special pad lodged between their knees can considerably ease back discomfort.

- If (as far as you know or from what your bed partner may have told you) you lie mostly on your back while you're asleep, you may find that you get a better night's rest by placing a pillow under your knees or supporting your legs from the knees down with cushions.

- If you spend any time awake in bed, do change positions now and then.
- Getting in and out of bed requires special care as it's quite easy to set off back pain by doing this too hastily. The NBPA recommends: "When getting into bed, sit on the edge, lower your body onto the elbow and shoulder, draw up your knees until your feet are on the mattress, then roll your body over to face the ceiling. Reverse the procedure when getting out – and bend both knees." Naturally, always move slowly and deliberately, and particularly so when getting up in the morning. Your back is often at its most vulnerable at that time because joints do tend to stiffen when they are not being used. While rest can help your spine in many ways, being mainly immobile while asleep can also leave it very stiff and perhaps painful when you wake.

SOME OTHER POINTS TO CONSIDER

While there is a direct correlation between your sleeping pattern and back pain and sciatica, how well you sleep is also likely to have a major effect on your overall health and stress levels, which in turn may also affect your back problems. Here are some extra facts about sleep that underline the importance of this often-neglected aspect of our lives:

- Most of us spend up to a third of each day in bed – that's about 29,200 hours in bed every ten years.
- New research has shown that people who try to cut down on sleep are more prone to infection and irritability. In a recent study of 9,000 British adults, it was found that those who slept between six-and-a-half and eight-and-a-half hours enjoyed much better overall health than those who slept for less.
- Lack of sleep can sabotage diets and knock our immune system

for six: exhausted people are far more likely to pick up bugs and infections because of the way lack of sleep upsets the normal cycle of chemical and hormone release.

- When a representative sample of more than 300 adults aged 30 to 60 years were asked about the effect a bad night's sleep had on them, 79 per cent of people saw a direct link between the way they had slept and how they felt the next day. A staggering 52 per cent said that they regularly experienced tiredness/lethargy, irritability, poor concentration, depression or headaches which they attributed to poor quality sleep.

- Only 10 per cent of people stated that they always had a good night's sleep – these were the people who regularly got more than the average amount of sleep.

- How much sleep do we really need? While this will vary greatly from person to person, the average amount of sleep needed each day, according to the *Ushborne Book of Body Facts,* is 16 to 20 hours for a new-born baby; 13 hours for a two-year-old; 10 to 11 hours for a five-year-old; 9 to 10 hours for a ten-year-old; 7 to 8 hours for an adult; and a mere 5 hours for an eighty-year-old. On the average, people sleep for just 6.7 hours before a working day and 7.1 hours before a day off.

CHAPTER 10

How reducing stress can alleviate back pain symptoms

Stress is a term that, according to its context, can have many different meanings, these including:

- A mentally or emotionally disruptive or upsetting condition occurring in response to adverse external influences and capable of affecting physical health, usually characterised by greater muscular tension, an increased heart rate, a rise in blood pressure, irritability, and possibly accompanied by depressive feelings.
- A stimulus or circumstance causing such a condition.
- A state of extreme difficulty, pressure, or strain – the latter, of course, also including chronic pain, such as that which may be suffered by someone with acute sciatica.

Additionally, of course, one needs to differentiate sharply between clearly obvious physical stress – such as that you may inflict on your back by, let's say, lifting a heavy object – and any mental stress that can colour how you may react to symptoms and therefore how painful these may feel.

Physical stress and how to avoid it making your condition worse has been dealt with in *Chapter 7*. However, we now look at the other kind of stress – the emotional kind – and how reducing or controlling this can in turn make your symptoms more bearable or even make it seem that they've disappeared altogether.

There is little doubt that how you experience pain or discomfort – or, perhaps more accurately, how you react to these – will often be strongly influenced by your state of mind at the time. A sciatic twinge or a tightness in the lower back will be all the more apparent and distressing when your spirits are at a low ebb than when you're feeling on top of the world. While your mental state may not affect your pain itself, it will certainly have a great effect upon how strongly you perceive it.

REDUCING STRESS CAN HELP IN MANY WAYS

Although experts may disagree about how much stress contributes to back troubles and its related symptoms, there are few who would not agree wholeheartedly that a carefully planned programme of stress reduction can be in the best long-term interests of any patient experiencing such difficulties.

When looking at the link between physical symptoms and mental stress, it's worth remembering how Dr Hans Selye, a world-renowned expert on the subject, who has been credited with the discovery of the concept of biological stress, explained it thus: "Stress is the non-specific response by the body to any demand." Putting this another way, it means that your body may react in ways that are totally unhelpful – such as your muscles getting all knotted up – when you're under stress.

WHAT'S YOUR STRESS LEVEL?

It's a fact that many highly-stressed individuals simply refuse to accept that they may be more stressed than is good for them; this denial, of course, allows them to ignore the situation and just carry on as before. But there is no question that all of us, no matter how much we may like to think that we're always totally in full control of our emotions, are to a greater or lesser degree susceptible to stress, either because we over-react to events or because we have a low stress tolerance level in the first instance.

Although a little bit of undue stress now and then may not do a great deal of harm, ongoing undue stress at a high level certainly will eventually exact a price to be paid in overall poorer health, whether this manifests itself as back pain or any one of a dozen other conditions whose incidence is at least partly linked to stress or worsened by it.

Doctors, of course, have many ways of determining whether someone is overstressed, but there is also a very simple and remarkably accurate way of finding this out for yourself and that is to just ask yourself whether you're under undue stress. If 'yes' is the answer that immediately springs to your mind in response to this self-questioning, then it is most likely that this will indeed be so. Equally, should your own self-assessment suggest that you're not particularly stressed, then that, too, is most likely to be the correct conclusion.

Naturally, how much stress you're under usually varies considerably from day to day, week to week, month to month, and year to year. Just because you're not feeling stressed at a given moment doesn't necessarily mean that your body isn't nevertheless paying a price for previous times when you might have been under a great deal of pressure.

Because stress is seldom constant in its intensity, many people fail to come up with either a clear-cut 'yes' or 'no' answer when they ask themselves whether they're stressed, instead saying things like, "Well, I do get stressed now and then, but I can cope with it and it doesn't bother me" or "No, I'm pretty sure that I'm not under great stress – well, perhaps now and then things do get on top of me."

When you try this self-test and find that your own answer sounds a bit like those above, then most experts would suggest that you are indeed at least partly affected by stress. And, if you're having back problems, then the chances are that somewhere along the way stress has made a considerable difference to how much these have affected you. If so, it follows logically that reducing or controlling your stress level in the future is likely either to reduce your back problems or at least make them more bearable.

HOW TO REDUCE STRESS

There are essentially two main ways of reducing stress:
1) To identify the sources of your stress and where possible seek either to reduce or eliminate these; and/or
2) To find ways to enable you to cope better with those sources of stress you can neither reduce nor avoid.

The most effective way to get your stress level down is usually by working towards both of these aims simultaneously. These tips from the experts will help you do just that:

- Much stress is linked to always being in a rush, to constantly fighting the clock to get everything you need to do completed in time. Plan your day more carefully, allow yourself enough time for what you must do and so meet deadlines more gracefully, and you'll find this cuts out a great deal of stress.

- Directly linked to the above is the recommendation that you should be careful not to set yourself unrealistic targets, especially those that you know beforehand you will probably be incapable of meeting or where you will only manage to do so by rushing like mad or cutting corners, this being a sure-fire recipe to push up your stress level.

- Always think things through carefully before you act or commit yourself to a course of action. Impulsive and less than well-thought-out actions are frequently the source of subsequent regrets, and the latter can be extremely stressful.

- Set aside time to relax both physically and mentally for at least a part of every day, no matter how busy your schedule may be.

- Retain control of your own life by learning to say 'no' if saying 'yes' would commit you to what is likely to become a stressful situation.

- Whenever possible, take a break now and then, as a change of routine can recharge your mental and emotional batteries and improve your resistance to stress, thereby effectively reducing your level of it.

- Learn to accept sensible limitations. If something is beyond your control, accept it as gracefully as possible until the time comes when you can do something to change it for the better. Agonising and worrying about things that can't be helped is a major cause of stress and can also be a precursor to chronic anxiety.

WHERE TO START

The sensible way to begin any programme to reduce your stress level is to identify as fully as possible all the various things that contributed to creating it in the first place.

Stressors – that's factors that cause stress – are divided into two main groups:

1) Stressors you can either avoid altogether or eliminate most of the time. For example, if you find that you always become highly irritated and 'up-tight' whenever you visit your in-laws, it would be sensible to perhaps see them less frequently; or if your temper rises to boiling point every time you can't find a place to park your car in town, consider going in by bus or train instead.

2) Stressors about which you can do little, or at least not in the short term, and which are essentially beyond your control. Typical stressors of this type include work problems, money worries, or deteriorating family and marital relationships.

Identify your own personal stressors by making a list of those events, situations, and other factors that you know make *you* feel stressed. In this list also include seemingly minor problems that bother you frequently as it's not uncommon for these – if they come up often – to be a cumulative source of stress whose total effect is considerably more powerful than you might expect.

Divide your list into two parts: the stressors you can avoid or eliminate and those which you'll have to grin and bear, at least for the immediately foreseeable future. Review your list carefully, considering each item in turn and thinking about what you can do about it to make things better for yourself. As you go through this exercise, you're likely to be surprised by how much stress you can avoid by making the simplest of adjustments to your lifestyle or environment. Naturally, you'll be reducing your total stress level every time you find a way to avoid or reduce the impact of a stressor.

Extremely useful though this eliminatory approach can be, it may still not be enough to bring your stress down to an acceptable level as there will probably still remain a number of major stressors which will not disappear or change overnight. What can be done, however, is to change the intensity with which you react to these 'permanent' stressors, so reducing their impact upon you and making their effects less harmful to you in the long term.

WHY RELAXATION IS BETTER THAN DRUGS

Although someone who is very stressed may need medication on a temporary basis to get them through a particularly sticky patch, this kind of treatment invariably involves its own risks, including those of potential side-effects as well as the danger of becoming dependent on the drugs. Tranquillisers were commonly prescribed – many experts say overprescribed – to combat stress until quite recently, but doctors are nowadays much more aware of the pitfalls of this approach and are instead choosing more and more to help stressed patients by using various 'relaxation techniques'.

There are many different types of these techniques, all of them sharing the same broad aim, but seeking to reach their goal in varying ways. Three techniques used frequently – and generally most successfully – to reduce stress that may be exacerbating muscular tension in general and back pain in particular are active relaxation, passive relaxation, and breath control, all of which can be used either individually or in any permutation with the other two.

Relaxation techniques produce tangible benefits in two quite distinct but interconnected ways:
1) They can prevent stress and/or tension from reaching such a point where they cause symptoms to appear.

2) When symptoms, such as sciatica, are already present, relaxation can help reduce them.

While it is not within the scope of this book to go into the various relaxation techniques in depth, there are many other books available that give simple step-by-step instructions. To help you make a start, there follows details of three simple methods for promoting relaxation that many people with back difficulties have found especially useful. First, however, a note of caution is in order: while all of these techniques are normally safe for anyone in reasonably good health, it is just possible that they could lead to an adverse effect under some circumstances. Therefore, should you try any of these methods, stop the exercise immediately if you feel at all uneasy at any time. And, to be absolutely safe, ask your doctor for his advice before you try these.

METHOD ONE – ACTIVE RELAXATION

This is probably the single most useful technique for bringing rapid relief from stress and also has the benefit that it is the most easy to learn and apply. Essentially, it consists of promoting mental relaxation through physical relaxation, the latter being attained through first deliberately tensing muscles and then consciously relaxing them.

Here's a very basic active relaxation programme which you can adapt as you wish to meet your own needs and circumstances:

- Select a time of day when you don't expect to be interrupted. Lie down flat on your back on the floor, placing a light support – a small cushion or a rolled up towel – under your head.
- Extend your legs fully, but spread slightly apart. Your arms should be at your sides, but also spread out slightly.
- Clear your mind of all other thoughts and concentrate solely on registering the sensations that will be fed back from various parts of your body as you alternatively contract – that is tense up – and then deliberately relax various muscle groups in your body.

Incidentally, never try to relax a muscle without contracting it first – by contracting the muscle first, you'll learn to recognise the contrast between a muscle that is tense and one that is fully relaxed. To make sure that a muscle is fully contracted, clench or tighten it hard for at least ten seconds before letting it go fully limp and resting loosely wherever it is, supported only by gravity.

This 'tense it up first, then relax it totally' procedure is carried out in sequence to extend to every major set of muscles in the body, starting with those that are furthest from your head. This is the sequence recommended by experts to attain the maximum amount of overall relaxation in the shortest time:

- Begin with your toes, tensing and relaxing each of them in turn. Then on to the feet, one at a time, then the calves, knees, thighs, and buttocks, alternating between your left and right sides until both your legs are totally relaxed.
- Next comes the trunk. Start with the lower abdomen, then the upper abdomen, followed by the lower back, the upper back, the chest and finally the shoulders.
- Now do the arms, starting once again with the muscles furthest away from your head. First the fingers, each individually of course, followed by the hands, wrists, forearms, and upper arms.
- Finally, it's the turn of the neck and head. Start with the neck, then the throat and lower jaw, finishing with the face. Contract each section of the face separately – that is chin, lips, cheeks, nose, forehead and eyes in turn.
- Once all the muscles in your body are fully relaxed, just lie still for ten minutes or so, enjoying the sensation of physical relaxation while keeping your mind clear of worries or problems.
- At the end of your allotted time, get up slowly and deliberately, not abruptly as this could cause the unnecessary contraction of muscles you've just relaxed.

Although this routine should ideally be performed daily, this may not always be possible. If so, do the exercise as often as you can, preferably at least three times a week. Incidentally, although it may take you twenty minutes or longer to work your way through the various sets of muscles at first, you will soon find that this speeds up immensely after you've done it a few times.

METHOD TWO – PASSIVE RELAXATION

This form of relaxation – also called meditative relaxation – addresses itself directly to your mind as you clear it of extraneous thoughts to concentrate on a single relaxing idea or image.

Passive relaxation will usually be most effective when it immediately follows a session of active relaxation, for example, such as the exercise described directly above. There is no specific position you should adopt for passive relaxation, but it's obviously important that you be at ease and comfortable, and you could either be sitting or lying down, whatever seems most suitable for you.

Start by spending a moment or two relaxing your body and clearing your mind before going on to the meditative process itself with one of the following methods:

- Close your eyes, then evoke a mental image of a place where you'd really like to be. The image you imagine can either be that of a real or totally imaginary place. For example, it could be a warm beach, a sunlit meadow, a mountain top, or whatever strikes your personal fancy. Use your mind's eyes and explore in depth all the pleasing aspects of this peaceful and wonderful place, absorbing and rejoicing in its sights, sounds and smells as you luxuriate and delight in being there. Eventually, bring yourself gradually back to reality, but hold on to the deep sense of inner peace and calm you experienced as you visited your mental paradise.

- While in a relaxed state, look at a previously chosen object you find really pleasing, such as a vase full of flowers, a statuette, or a painting. Bring all your senses to bear fully on this object: your eyes noting its every intricate detail; your hands gently exploring its shape, contours and textures; and your mind responding to the beauty of every pleasing pattern it recognises. Spend a few minutes on this mental inventory, then close your eyes and re-create the object in your mind while you think about all its beautiful aspects.

METHOD THREE – BREATH CONTROL

Both of the two relaxation promoting methods described above can be used most successfully with additional exercises in which you exercise conscious control over your breathing. Breath control can not only help you relax even more deeply, but it also revitalises your whole body by providing it with an extra intake of oxygen that 'recharges' your whole organism.

Of the many different kinds of breathing exercises, the single most useful one is the *Complete Breath*, a technique that comes from ancient Hatha Yoga, that part of Yoga discipline concerned with the control of the physical body. An excellent time to use the *Complete Breath* is while you're still lying down after completing a relaxation exercise. Here's what you do:

- Bring your legs and feet together so that they nearly touch, leaving your arms lying loosely at your sides.
- Very slowly and deliberately, take in a deep breath and while doing so gradually raise your hands upwards to initially make them meet above your head, then move them back further so that they end up lying straight out behind your head with their palms up.
- Now exhale slowly and deliberately, fully emptying your lungs, and as you do so bring your arms back to where they were originally along your sides.
- Repeat this procedure up to ten times, making certain that each successive cycle proceeds smoothly into the next one. It's most important not to hurry this exercise, but to concentrate on making each movement as smooth as possible, letting it flow naturally into the one that follows.

The above are, of course, just a few of the many proven relaxation techniques available. Many more are an essential part of the therapies offered by alternative practitioners, details of which can be found in *Chapter 12 – More alternative treatments that can help.*

CHAPTER 11

Problems at work

While it's up to you to make sure that you take sensible precautions at home to protect your health, it's a different matter when you're at work where the demands of the job or the facilities provided for doing it can force you into a situation where damage to your back can result.

Sciatica and back pain are. of course, part of a much wider range of, at times, work-related ailments of all kinds that fall under the broad label of 'musculoskeletal disorders', a term that encompasses those conditions that affect the bones and muscles of the body and the tissues that hold them together.

Musculoskeletal problems often arise from tasks performed while employed, and each year more than half a million cases are reported as being caused by work. Says the Health and Safety Executive (HSE): "The potential to cause these conditions exists in most workplaces – although certain types of work are more often associated with musculoskeletal disorders than others, such as poultry processing, clothing manufacture, keyboard operation, nursing and assembly line work."

According to the HSE, the causes fall into three main categories:

- **Manual handling and lifting** – poorly designed tasks and incorrect lifting techniques and posture all increase the risk to workers. More than 55,000 injuries due to handling, lifting or carrying accidents are reported yearly.
- **Repetitive work** – where work is done too quickly, such as in piecework, or where the work rate is controlled by a machine. This can be a particular problem when combined with the need

for force; where the operator is positioned badly; or where the job is not varied enough.

- **Unsuitable posture** – often caused by poor seating arrangements or by reaching and stretching awkwardly.

While a specific injury to the affected part can be detected in many instances of work-related disorders, in others, pain and discomfort may be the only evidence of problems, as in the case of chronic back pain or sciatica.

The HSE firmly believes that most of these problems can be avoided, often through relatively simple corrective action, such as perhaps modifying how a job is performed, or through re-siting parts of machinery or adapting seating positions.

The responsibility for preventing health problems caused by working conditions is one that is shared to a large extent by both the employee and the employer, and these can be summed up as follows:

- The employer has a legal duty to safeguard the employee's health and safety, and should identify tasks which could cause problems and take steps to improve the situation.
- The employee must, however, exercise care and follow good work practices, particularly where lifting and carrying are involved. It is also up to the employee to ensure that any workstation is correctly adjusted when adequate adjustment is possible.

Spelling this out more fully, current relevant legislation includes:

- Section 2 of the *Health and Safety at Work etc Act 1974 (HSW Act)* which places a duty on employers to ensure, so far as is reasonably practicable, the health, safety and welfare at work of all their employees.
- Section 6 of this Act also places a duty on manufacturers, designers, suppliers and importers of articles for use at work to ensure, so far as is reasonably practicable, that the article is so designed and constructed as to be safe and without risks to health.
- Under section 7 of the Act, employees have to take reasonable care for their own health and safety and that of others who may be affected by what they do (or fail to do); they also have to

cooperate with their employer, so far as is necessary, to enable the employer to comply with legal duties.

It must be noted that the HSW Act deals with general duties and does not provide specific requirements on the prevention of particular ailments. However, various Regulations are more to the point as far as reducing the risk of back pain or injury are concerned, as shown below.

The Management of Health and Safety at Work Regulations 1992 (the Management Regulations) include requirements for employers to:

- Assess risks to health or safety.
- Arrange for the effective planning, organisation, control, monitoring and review of preventive and protective measures.
- Appoint competent people to assist the employer in complying with health and safety law.
- Cooperate and coordinate health and safety actions where the activities of different employers interact.
- Provide appropriate health surveillance, information and training.

The Provision and Use of Work Equipment Regulations 1992 place duties on employers concerning the safe and proper use of work equipment. The risk assessment carried out under the Management Regulations, as mentioned above, is intended to help employers select work equipment and assess its suitability.

The Health and Safety (Display Screen Equipment) Regulations 1992 are directed mainly to protect employees who habitually use display screen equipment as a significant part of their normal work. Employers have duties to:

- Assess and reduce risks.
- Make sure new workstations meet minimum requirements covering equipment, furniture, the working environment, task design and software. There was a transition period until 31 December 1996 for existing workstations
- Provide breaks or changes of activity, information and training.

While the health risks most commonly associated with operating computers and other VDUs are upper limb disorders (including repetitive strain injury) and sight problems, back troubles can easily arise from inadequate seating and a lack of breaks in the day's work.

The Manual Handling Operations Regulations 1992 require the avoidance or reduction of risk where the manual handling of loads involves a risk of injury.

The Workplace (Health, Safety and Welfare) Regulations 1992 include requirements for lighting, workspace, workstation arrangements, seating and facilities for rest.

The Supply of Machinery (Safety) Regulations 1992 apply to the supply of new machinery which will need to meet relevant essential health and safety requirements.

Taken together, the HSW Act and the various Regulations put a strong onus upon any employer to ensure that everything reasonable be done to prevent employees from contracting work-related ailments. Despite that, it remains a fact that many sufferers from back problems certainly attribute their difficulties to conditions at work. Should you think that your health problems are due to unsatisfactory work practices, this is what the HSE says you should do:

- In the first instance, consult your doctor, giving as much information as is possible to enable him to decide whether or not your condition is likely to be due to your work. In some cases individuals suffering from specified conditions can get state compensation under the *Industrial Injuries Prescribed Diseases Regulations*. Ask your doctor about this or get *leaflet N12* from your nearest Social Security office.

- If you suffer from symptoms which may be attributable to work, particularly if they recur, then it is important to tell your doctor and employer. If you have a works nurse or doctor, then you should also tell them about your problem. You may also want your union representative to know that you think your job is affecting you. If you are off sick for more than seven days your doctor will inform your employer of the cause via a sick note.

- You can also contact a doctor or nurse from your local Employment Medical Advisory Service. You'll find them at your local office of the Health and Safety Executive.
- If you need more information, contact the *HSE's Information Centre* on 0541 545500.

Additionally, should you develop a musculoskeletal disorder that makes it difficult for you to continue with your current job or you are out of work, you can get advice from your local Job Centre on assessment and rehabilitation schemes, registration as a disabled person, job retention, work aids for people with disabilities and help with job applications.

A NOTE FOR EMPLOYERS

While meeting the requirements of the various regulations may at times be expensive, it obviously makes good sense for employers to do so because otherwise the serious ill effects of work-related disorders can also lead to high costs. The HSE points out that these costs can include:
- Sick pay, loss of production due to poor performance, sickness absence and poor industrial relations; and
- Possible compensation payments. Considerable sums have been won in civil claims and this may increase the cost of Employers' Liability Compulsory Insurance.

To reduce the risk of work-related disorders, the HSE recommends that employers should:
- Make sure that work systems cater for the differences in people's size, strength and abilities. Wherever possible allow people some control over work speed.
- Think about any possible risks when planning changes to work methods or when buying new machinery or equipment. Check with suppliers that ergonomic principles have been incorporated in the design of new equipment.
- Consider a programme of 'health surveillance'. This could

include a system for keeping records of problems when they first appear and for prompt medical assessment to anyone reporting problems. Encourage early reporting of symptoms (a positive safety culture will help) and look at sickness absence records and staff turnover.

- Look into the possibility of alternative work or job changes when someone cannot continue their current type of work or where this will aid the return to work of someone who has been off sick.
- Monitor as frequently as necessary to check the effectiveness of your control measures. Look, for example, to possible adjustment of workstations and seating, working techniques, maintenance arrangements. Be alert to any increase in work-related ailments in the workplace, for example, after a change of process, speed or working technique.
- Finally, review your arrangements periodically.

FOR MORE INFORMATION

Safety at work is, of course, a vast subject. For more detailed information consult the following HSE books and leaflets which you can order from *HSE Books* on 01787 881165:

Seating at work; *Lighting at work*; *Ergonomics at work*; *Working with VDUs*; *Lighten the load: guidance for employers on musculoskeletal disorders*; *Management of health and safety at work*; *Approved code of practice*; *Work equipment: guidance on regulations*; *Manual handling: guidance on regulations*; *Workplace health, safety and welfare: approved code of practice*; *Display screen equipment work: guidance on regulations*.

CHAPTER 12

More alternative treatments that can help

In *Chapter 5* we looked at those complementary and alternative therapies that are used so commonly to treat back troubles that many of them can almost be considered as part and parcel of conventional medicine as far as these specific problems are concerned. There are, however, also many other alternative therapies that can help in certain situations and these are described in this chapter. But first, let's consider why sufferers may turn away from what can be called the 'mainstream' therapies to try others, whose record although good, has less documented evidence to back up their efficacy.

Many forms of back problems, including sciatica, while chronic, do tend to come and go, waxing and waning in intensity with there often being little obvious reason why suddenly there is a worsening or improvement in the condition. While the correct treatment, coupled with sensible lifestyle adjustments and the taking of proper precautions will usually bring great relief from any acute attack of back trouble, this does not necessarily mean that any underlying condition has been cured permanently. As most back pain sufferers will testify, once you have had the problem you're always going to be particularly susceptible of it happening again.

Because people with back problems don't always get all the help they would hope for from conventional medicine, it's not surprising that many of them eventually turn to practitioners of alternative medicine. There are many reasons why this should happen, but these are the main ones, according to a recent survey:

- Patients often feel that their family doctors do not treat them with the seriousness that they feel their symptoms deserve. In fact, once the possibility of any dangerous underlying condition has been eliminated, doctors can be somewhat dismissive of what they consider to be 'minor' back problems, saying, more or less, that it's up to the patient to take the recommended steps to avoid the symptoms. Many of these recommendations are, however, sometimes a whole lot easier to offer than to follow, and a patient may well feel that his doctor has 'abandoned' him after offering the minimum advice.

- While specific attacks of sciatica or other symptoms of back trouble occur because of a direct cause at the time, there is nevertheless often little obvious reason why the problem should be so much worse during one period of time than another. As we've already discussed previously, this 'waxing and waning' can be at times directly attributed to greater or lesser stress. Conventional Western medicine is by no means always terribly successful in dealing with ongoing and changing personal problems that exacerbate physical problems, leaving sufferers to wonder whether they might fare better with other therapies.

- Busy family doctors, especially in today's over-worked National Health Service, tend to look primarily at physical causes, and patients may feel that a better overall solution to their problems may be found by alternative practitioners because they usually focus their attention on what they call the 'whole person', and not just the particular complaint being presented.

- Another prevalent reason for seeking alternative help is because the patient may be desperate for improvement. When this doesn't seem to be forthcoming from conventional medicine, despite his having tried all it had to offer, he will then quite reasonably also look elsewhere for help.

- Some patients also turn to alternative medicine, especially to those disciplines that preach 'mind over matter', for help in complying with some of the health recommendations they have received from their doctor. For example, a patient may find it easier to lose weight when supported in his attempt by some alternative therapies, especially those that concentrate on developing the power of self-suggestion.

Other reasons why alternative or complementary practitioners can help include:

- The mere fact of consulting an alternative practitioner can in itself make a patient treat more seriously the recommendations he receives that way. It's a fact that when you have to pay for advice, you tend to listen to it more carefully than when it comes free. The additional motivation this effect can produce may at times be enough to allow a patient to do all that's needed to bring about an improvement, such as taking the right kind of exercises, losing weight, and so on.

- One more important reason why alternative therapy may at times be more successful than conventional medicine is that many of the techniques commonly used by alternative practitioners are specifically devised to increase a patient's confidence in himself and his own ability to take the necessary steps to bring his condition under control, or to, at least, be less affected by the symptoms when they occur.

While there's a great deal to be said in favour of alternative medicine, it must be pointed out that patients would always be well-advised in being extremely cautious in deciding whether to follow this course and, if so, how to go about it. These tips will guide you:

- Before seeking help from other sources you should always see your own doctor first to ensure a proper diagnosis is made initially. This is absolutely vital, if only so that other possibly more serious reasons for your symptoms can be safely excluded. It might also be useful to ask your doctor whether he believes that one or another form of alternative medicine could help you; not all doctors have closed minds about the possible benefits of alternative approaches to treatment.

- Should you decide on a course of alternative therapy, you should immediately consult your doctor once again if any new symptoms were to develop or if your existing ones were to become more severe or frequent while you were being treated by someone else. What's more, it's also a good idea to check out with your doctor the safety aspects of any alternative treatments you're offered.

As far as choosing a specific therapist is concerned, do make sure that it's a properly-trained and reputable one. These suggestions will help you do just that:

- Make sure that the alternative practitioner of your choice is a fully accredited member of a professional body whose standing is generally recognised.

- While medical doctors usually aren't keen to recommend alternative practitioners, it's quite possible that your family doctor may be willing to do exactly that, but you may perhaps have to read somewhat between the lines of what you're told. The positive contribution that alternative practitioners can make in some instances has received wider acceptance from mainstream medicine in recent years.

- Personal recommendations from people whose judgement you trust are another excellent guide.

Which particular alternative therapy might be worth a try is largely a matter of individual choice, each and every one of them having their ardent supporters. Here to help you make your choice are brief details of the main ones most likely to be able to help with sciatica or other back problems.

HOMOEOPATHY

Almost without a doubt the most universally accepted form of alternative therapy, homoeopathy is a treatment system developed in the late 18th century by Samuel Hahnemann, a German doctor. The basis of the therapy is enshrined in two main guiding principles: first, that 'like cures like'; and, secondly, that 'less is more'. What this means in practice is that homoeopathic remedies for a given condition are often derived from the very elements believed to have brought on the ailment in the first place, and that these remedies will be administered in an extremely minimal dosage.

Homoeopathy also embraces two further beliefs:

1) Symptoms are signs produced by the body as part of its efforts to ward off or reduce the effects of infection or disease; and

2) The body has the ability to cope with most illnesses, and the doctor's main job is to help strengthen that ability.

To aid and stimulate the body's natural defence systems, treatments are usually administered as very small doses of various preparations, these being taken either as tablets or as liquids, which are prepared from natural substances and originate from various herbal, animal, mineral and metallic sources. In keeping with the principle that 'less is more', the remedies are invariably supplied in so diluted a form that just about none of the original healing ingredient can still be detected in the final mixture, something which, of course, has raised the question of how can a remedy possibly have any useful therapeutic effect is there is nothing – or very little – left in it of the active ingredient? Homoeopathic practitioners are the first to admit that they, too, can't fully explain why such highly-diluted preparations should work, but point out that there's plenty of accumulated scientific evidence to prove beyond a doubt that it does in many cases.

Homoeopathy is an alternative therapy that is also used quite frequently by some medically qualified doctors and, under certain circumstances, it may even be available free through the National Health Service.

Because they are so diluted, you don't need a prescription to buy homoeopathic remedies, and you can get these over the counter in most pharmacies and health stores. Although this easy availability of homoeopathic preparations might tempt someone to choose his own remedy, practitioners caution against this, pointing out that it takes a great deal of skill and experience to choose the right one for any given situation.

In fact, a quick look in *The Prescriber*, which is a kind of mini-Bible listing the main homoeopathic preparations, will give some idea of how many different remedies there are for what is essentially the same ailment. For example, under the heading 'sciatica' you will find many different suggestions, according to whether the condition is 'in young people, and from cold draughts', or whether 'the pain increases when sitting, is relieved somewhat by walking, or entirely by lying down'. Other factors taken into consideration are whether the symptoms are better or worse at night or when resting, what times of day it occurs, whether chronic or acute, accompanied by cramps or alternating with numbness, or felt as a drawing, tearing, shooting or paralytic pain. Check under 'back pain' and you'll find that the recommended remedy also depends upon a similarly wide variety of factors. Clearly, faced with such a multitude of potential remedies, selecting the right one is something beyond the scope of most laymen and best left to an expert.

You can get more information about homoeopathy from: *The British Homoeopathic Association*, 27a Devonshire Street, London W1N 1RJ; *The Homoeopathic Society*, Hahnemann House, 2 Powis Place, Great Ormond Street, London WC1N 3HT; *The Society of Homoeopaths*, 2 Artizan Road, Northampton NN1 4HU.

NATUROPATHY

Also known as 'naturopathic medicine', naturopathy is an extremely broadly-based system of medicine that combines a wide variety of natural therapeutic and healing techniques under one umbrella, and it can perhaps be best described as a mixture of traditional folk wisdom and modern medicine. The main underlying principle of this alternative therapy is that the root-cause of all disease is the accumulation of waste products and toxins within the human body, this usually being the result of a lifestyle that is 'deficient'.

Like homoeopaths, naturopaths believe that the human body has the innate wisdom and power to heal itself, providing we enhance rather than interfere with this power. As far as actual treatments are concerned, naturopathy relies heavily on herbal preparations and diet management techniques, but depending upon his training, a naturopath may offer any – or even all – of the following therapies: physiotherapy, this based on water, ultrasound, heat or cold; yoga or other breathing exercises; biofeedback techniques; corrective nutrition; as well as many others.

Naturopaths rely heavily upon the practitioner and the patient discussing and agreeing upon what therapies should be used. There is also much emphasis upon the promotion of psychological health and the benefits of stress reduction. Generally, this is an alternative therapy that has a good track record in helping people with chronic ailments of all kinds, especially when the symptoms arise from or are made worse by tension, anxiety or stress.

You can get more information from: *The General Council and Register of Naturopaths*, Goswell House, 2 Goswell Road, Street, Somerset BA16 0JG; *The Natural and Therapeutic and Osteopathic Society and Register*, 14 Marford Road, Wheathampstead, Herts AL4 8AS.

HYPNOSIS AND HYPNOTHERAPY

These are two forms of treatment that are used quite commonly by both medical doctors as well as by alternative practitioners. Although these therapies would seem at first to have but little role to play in managing sciatica and back problems, they can help in a variety of ways, including:

- They can help a patient bring about lifestyle changes indicated for improving his condition. For example, hypnosis can help someone stick to a diet.
- Affect how the patient looks at and reacts to his difficulties. While hypnosis may perhaps make no difference to the extent of sciatica,

it certainly can alter the way someone reacts to it when it happens, either by making him less aware of it or by increasing his level of tolerance to it.

- These therapies are also particularly useful for reducing stress and anxiety, these often being an exacerbating factor in all kinds of back-connected problems.

Hypnosis and hypnotherapy both depend on the power of suggestion, whether the suggestions originate from the practitioner or the patient himself. In fact, it is generally believed that no one is ever hypnotised by anyone else, and that what invariably happens is that the subject hypnotises himself, the hypnotist merely providing a conduit for this self-hypnosis.

Not every patient is a suitable subject for this approach, and there is considerable individual variation in the extent to which people respond to this technique, some falling almost immediately into a deep trance-like state at the first suggestion while others totally fail to respond. There is, however, no need for a subject to attain a deep hypnotic state before hypnosis can work, the very lightest of trances being enough to achieve results.

Hypnosis can be tried out at very little cost and with minimal risk by buying one or more of the self-hypnosis tapes that are commonly advertised in newspapers and magazines. These tapes, of course, are usually aimed at creating generally beneficial effects – such as inducing relaxation or reducing reaction to pain – but often can be adapted by the user so that the suggestions they contain become directly relevant to the problem. Many hypnotists will also provide patients with individualised tapes they can later use at home to reinforce suggestions made during previous treatment sessions.

For more information contact: *The British Society of Hypnotherapists*, 37 Orbain Road, Fulham, London SW6 7JZ; *The International Association of Hypnotherapists*, 1 Lowther Gardens, Bournemouth, Dorset DH8 8NH; *The National Council of Psychotherapists and Hypnotherapists Register*, 46 Oxhey Road, Oxhey, Watford, Herts

WD1 4QQ; *British Hypnosis Research*, 8 Paston Place, Brighton, East Sussex BN2 2HA; *The National Register of Hypnotherapists and Psychotherapists*, 12 Cross Street, Nelson, Lancashire BB9 7EN.

HERBALISM

Probably the oldest form of medicine, herbalism – also known as 'herbal medicine' – has a history going back at least 3,000 years. First developed in ancient China, herbalism is based on the therapeutic uses of various plant parts – root, bark, stem, flowers, leaf, and even seeds – in different preparations, either for internal or external use as teas, potions, juice extracts, bath additives, salve, lotions, and ointments.

Throughout the ages there has always been a strong association between herbal remedies and back problems of all kinds. Modern herbalists believe that medicines are not just only a means of treating illness, but are also a way of restoring the body's balance to its normal state, disease or pain being viewed by them as 'abnormal states'. Of course, this approach means that a given disorder may not always be treated by the same herbal preparation, as deciding what the right treatment is in a given case will also take into account several other factors, including the patient's general health, disposition, and even personality. However, in making their choices, practitioners are guided by *pharmacopoeias* – these being comprehensive listings of remedies that have proven themselves useful in specific conditions – and some of these have origins going back more than 6,000 years, having been first formulated when the Chinese started classifying and cataloguing herbal cures.

Although herbalism has helped many people suffering from chronic conditions such as sciatica or back pain, a note of caution is in order: herbal preparations can be just as powerful – and therefore potentially also as toxic – as modern day drugs. This means that these remedies have to be prescribed and used with the greatest of care as they can lead to serious side-effects. It is essential therefore that herbal remedies should be prescribed by and used under the supervision of a suitably qualified medical herbalist.

You can get more information from: *The National Institute of Medical Herbalists*, 56 Longbrook Street, Exeter, Devon EX4 6AH.

OTHER ALTERNATIVE THERAPIES

The therapies above, although part of 'alternative medicine', are nevertheless so well-established that they are often seen as an adjunct to conventional treatment rather than an alternative to it. There are, however, also several other therapies which while less generally accepted have helped at least some people suffering from chronic conditions, although there is very little or no creditable scientific evidence available either to prove their effectiveness or exactly how they work. Here are brief details of some of these methods – do, however, please remember that the mention of a therapy here is not meant to be interpreted as an endorsement of it.

AROMATHERAPY

This form of treatment is based on the use of essential oils – these derived from wild or cultivated plants, herbs, fruits, and tress – to restore the body's natural functions and rhythms. The essences are prepared in many different ways: as compresses, bath additives, inhalants, and massaging lubricants.

Aromatherapists say they can help people with back problems in two main ways: either by using the essences to treat the problem directly by using them in massage sessions, or to control and reduce tension, anxiety and stress.

As with herbalism, a word of caution is in order: some of the aromatic oils are in fact poisonous in other than the very smallest quantities, and it is therefore absolutely essential that this therapy be administered by a qualified practitioner.

For more information contact: *International Federation of Aromatherapists*, 2-4 Chiswick High Road, London W4 1TH; *The*

International Society of Professional Aromatherapists, 82 Ashby Road, Hinckley, Leicestershire LE10 1SN; *The Tisserand Association of Holistic Aromatherapy*, 65 Church Road, Hove, East Sussex BN3 2BD.

BACH FLOWER REMEDIES

The Flower Remedies were created during the 1930s by Dr Edward Bach, a noted homoeopathic physician and bacteriologist, to treat 'emotional imbalances'. Although originally formulated primarily to supplement homoeopathic preparations, the remedies have since been used for all kinds of health problems. Similar to the Flower Remedies – of which there are 38 different varieties, all created by Dr Bach – are the Flower Essences which were developed later by followers of Dr Bach.

Much of the evidence about the efficacy of these remedies is anecdotal, but many people with back problems have reported that their symptoms were eased by the formulations. While the remedies are available without prescription in many health shops and pharmacies, it is no easy matter to select the right one, and it is therefore best to first consult a qualified practitioner.

For more information contact: *The Edward Bach Centre*, Mount Vernon, Sotwell, Wallingford, Oxon OX10 0PZ.

AUTOGENIC TRAINING AND THERAPY

This consists of a series of exercises aimed at generating a state of both mental and physical relaxation. It also includes some aspects of self-hypnosis in which the subjects use their own mind power to send themselves positive, healing messages about their condition. It is a 'mind-over-matter' approach that straddles that ill-defined border between hypnosis and meditation, both of which are altered mind states.

Many people with chronic pain and/or back problems have said that autogenic training had helped, both in dealing with immediate symptoms as well as reducing the stress that often had contributed to bringing these about.

For more information contact your doctor or local health centre.

SUMMING IT UP

The success – whether real or possibly imagined – of many alternative therapies often depends greatly upon the link between mental and physical well-being, a link that's also accepted by conventional medicine. Whether any of these alternative therapies are likely to help you is very much an individual judgement you must make for yourself, but ideally reaching your decision with the benefit of your own doctor's advice.

Additional sources of help and information

NATIONAL CHARITIES

The National Back Pain Association, 16 Elmtree Road, Teddington, Middlesex TW11 8ST. Tel: 0181 977 5474; Fax: 0181 943 5318.

The NBPA is a registered medical charity. It defines its mission as: running patient-orientated scientific research into the causes and treatments of back pain; to educate people to use their bodies sensibly, and thus reduce the incidence of back pain; to help fund and support Branches through which back pain sufferers and those who care for them may receive information, advice and mutual help.

Ordinary Membership: individuals £15.00 pa; families £20.00 pa; overseas £20.00 pa.

Special Membership (for those receiving state benefits or pensions): individuals £7.50 pa; families £10.00 pa.

If you join the NBPA, you will:

- Receive their informative and very readable quarterly magazine *TalkBack*. It keeps you up to date with back research and new products, tells you about special NBPA events such as their 'Back Pain Week' held every October, explains different types of treatment, and gives you an opportunity to communicate your own thoughts, experiences and ideas.
- Be invited to join one of the NBPA's local branches in an area

near you. Branches offer a variety of events, talks and get-togethers, and mutual support from other back pain sufferers.

- Be able to participate, if you wish, in decisions about how best to fight back pain by being able to vote at the NBPA's Annual General Meetings.
- Be part of the only charity working solely for back pain sufferers.

Professional Membership: UK £25.00 pa; overseas £30.00 pa. Open to members of the orthodox and complementary medical professions and all professionals with an interest in back pain Professional members receive an NBPA certificate, a special supplement to *TalkBack* and their names and contact details are added to the list of Professional Members, which is circulated to enquirers.

The Arthritis and Rheumatism Council for Research (ARC), Copeman House, St Mary's Court, St Mary's Gate, Chesterfield, Derbyshire S41 7TD. Tel: 01246 558033.

This national charity provides more than £10 million a year for rheumatology research into the causes and treatment of arthritis and rheumatism. It also produces an excellent range of leaflets and booklets about various aspects of these diseases.

PAIN CONTROL AND RELIEF

Pain Concern (UK), PO Box 318, Canterbury, Kent CT2 0GD. A registered charity concerned with providing information and support to all chronic pain sufferers and those caring for them, Pain Concern strives to raise awareness of the physical, mental, economic and spiritual needs of people in chronic pain throughout the United Kingdom.

It operates two special telephone services on 01227 264677:

- **The Information Line.** Available between the hours of 10 am and 4 pm, Bank Holidays excepted. A specially trained nurse is available to give you advice and information regarding all aspects of chronic pain. While this nurse cannot diagnose your problem, you can receive information of what services are available within the NHS and the private sector. Advice can also be given about complementary therapies which may be of help to you in controlling your chronic pain. The nurse at the end of the phone will have personal experience of chronic pain and has been specially trained to offer you advice on self-help. She/he will be able to give information on medicines and diet. The nurse will also be able to help you prepare for a consultation with your doctor by listening to your questions and helping you prepare a history of your problems.

- **The Listening Ear Helpline.** Available on the same number and at the same times as the Information Line, this helpline puts you in contact with a volunteer with personal experience of chronic pain who is available to offer sympathy, support and empathy to the enquirer. No medical or nursing advice will be available from these volunteers, but the opportunity to speak with a non-professional pain sufferer may also be of help. It may transpire during this contact that you need to speak with the nurse, so you will be given details of the times to ring for this specialist help from the volunteer.

Membership of Pain Concern (UK) is open to all and is currently £6.50 per annum. All members are sent four newsletters a year as well as an extensive fact-sheet. The fact-sheet can be obtained by non-members by sending a cheque or postal order for £1 payable to Pain Concern (UK) to the address on page 99.

The Pain Society, The British and Irish Chapter of the International Association for the Study of Pain, 9 Bedford Square, London WC1B 3RA. Tel: 0171 636 2750.

The Pain Society began as the Intractable Pain Society of Great Britain and Ireland in 1967, the first Society concerned with the clinical management of chronic pain. Membership was limited primarily to anaesthetists managing Pain Clinics but the Society also included consultant psychiatrists, neurosurgeons and neurologists.

The purposes for which the Society is organised are to relieve the suffering of pain by the promotion of education, research and training in the raising of standards in the management of pain.

Recognising that this goal could only be attained as a joint and interactive effort involving basic scientists and health care professionals, the Society has expanded in recent years to include all those with a professional commitment to pain. In recognition of this wider aim it has become The Pain Society.

While the Society welcomes general enquiries from the public on pain-related matters, it stresses that it cannot comment on individual cases. Referral to the nearest hospital Pain Clinic run by a member of the Society can be recommended only through a patient's General Practitioner or Hospital Consultant.

COMPLEMENTARY AND ALTERNATIVE THERAPIES

For more details of the therapies listed below, see *Chapter 5 – Other effective treatments for pain and sciatica.*

PHYSIOTHERAPY

The Chartered Society of Physiotherapy, 14 Bedford Row, London WC1R 4ED. Tel: 0171 306 6666.

Details of chartered physiotherapists in your area can be obtained from this organisation.

OSTEOPATHY

Osteopathy is a distinct system of diagnosis and treatment which is complementary to orthodox medicine. Osteopaths work with their hands using a range of treatment techniques. There are now over 2,000 osteopaths working all around the UK treating a wide variety of conditions, especially including pain in the lower back, tension headaches and many types of joint strain.

To find an osteopath near you: look in the *Yellow Pages, Thomson Directories* or ring *Talking Pages*; enquire at your health centre; ask your doctor; check the notice-board at your local library; ask at the Citizens Advice Bureau.

All qualified osteopaths will have an academic qualification indicated by DO (for Diploma of Osteopathy) or BSc (Ost) (for a degree in Osteopathy) after their name. Other letters after an osteopath's name usually indicate membership of one of the following registering bodies. The following organisations may be contacted directly for a list of members practising in your area:

- *General Council & Register of Osteopaths,* 56 London Street, Reading, Berkshire RG1 4SQ. Tel: 01734 576585. Members have MRO after their name.
- *The College of Osteopaths Practitioners' Association,* 13 Furzehill Road, Borehamwood, Hertfordshire WD6 2DG. Tel : 0181 905 1937. Members have MCO or FCO after their name.
- *Natural Therapeutic and Osteopathic Society and Register,* 63 Collingwood Road, Witham, Essex CM8 2EE. Members have MNTOS or FNTOS after their name.
- *The Guild of Osteopaths,* 497 Bury New Road, Prestwich, Manchester M25 1AD. Tel: 0161 798 6352. Members have MGO or FGO after their name.

CHIROPRACTIC

British Chiropractic Association, 29 Whitley Street, Reading, Berks RG2 0EG. Tel: 01734 757557.

Contact them for details of chiropractors in your area.

ACUPUNCTURE AND ACUPRESSURE

For more information contact: *The British Medical Acupuncture Society,* Newton House, Newton Lane, Lower Whitely, WAD 4JA; *The Council for Acupuncture,* 179 Gloucester Place, London NW1 6DX; *The Association of Chinese Acupuncture (College of Oriental Medicine),* Prospect House, 2 Grove Lane, Retford, Nottingham BN22 6NA; *The British Acupuncture Association,* 34 Alderney Street, London SW1V 4EU; *The Register of Chinese Medicine,* 19 Trinity Road, London N2 8JJ; *The Traditional Acupuncture Society,* 11 Grange Park, Stratford-upon-Avon, Warwickshire CV37 6HX.

FLOATATION

Details of centres offering floatation therapy can be obtained from: *Float Tank Association (UK),* PO Box 11024, London SW4 7ZF. Tel: 0171 627 4962.

YOGA

For more information contact: *The British Wheel of Yoga*, 1 Hamilton Place, Boston Road, Sleaford, Lincolnshire NG34 7ES; *The Yoga for Health Foundation,* Ickwell Bury, Northill, Biggleswade, Bedfordshire SG18 9EF.

THE ALEXANDER TECHNIQUE

For more information contact: *Society of Teachers of Alexander Technique,* London House, 266 Fulham Road, London SW10 9EL; *The Professional Association of Alexander Teachers*, Madian, Iorwerth Avenue, Aberystwyth, Dyfed SY23 1EW.

OTHER SOURCES OF INFORMATION

The Sleep Council

Good quality sleep is vital to us all, and in an ideal world we would all get the sleep we need but sometimes this is easier said than done. Your sleep can be affected by a variety of factors including worries, stress, your partner snoring, noises around you or even the quality of the bed.

Now help is at hand from an organisation called The Sleep Council which was formed to raise awareness of the benefits to health and well-being of quality sleep, enhanced by the support and comfort of a good bed, regularly replaced.

The Sleep Council has produced the *Sleep Good Feel Good Guide*, a handy leaflet filled with tips to help you get a good night's sleep. The leaflet also features a simple MOT (Mattress Obsolescence Test) that you can carry out to see if your bed could be affecting your quality of sleep. For anyone considering buying a new bed, the leaflet offers practical advice on how to choose a bed which will provide correct support.

The free *Sleep Good Feel Good Guide* can be obtained from your local Sleep Council stockist or by sending a stamped addressed envelope to The Sleep Council, High Corn Mill, Chapel Hill, Skipton, North Yorkshire, BD23 1NL.

MEDesign Ltd, Clock Tower Works, Railway Street, Southport, Merseyside PR8 5BB. Tel: 01704 542373; Fax: 01704 545214. This mail order supplier offers a wide range of special products to help back sufferers, including the Backfriend, an additional support that can be used with most chairs and car seats, as well as bed-boards, footrests, special pillows, and other useful aids. Contact them for a free copy of their *Back Pack* catalogue.

The Back Shop, 14 New Cavendish Street, London W1M 7LJ. Tel: 0171 935 9120; Fax: 0171 224 1903.

The Back Shop offers both products and expertise to help back sufferers at home, at work, at leisure and in the car.

A wide range of goods are on display at their New Cavendish Street showroom, where the staff are always ready to help you find the right solution for your back care problem. Alternatively, contact them for details of their mail order service.

They also offer a free posture assessment, a personal service designed to provide you with the maximum in practical comfort, and identify the most comfortable and supportive environment to prevent undue strain on the back. To arrange an appointment, please call Bonnie Mounayer or Zahid Malik on 0171 935 9120.